Song of Songs

INTERPRETATION
A Bible Commentary for Teaching and Preaching

INTERPRETATION
A BIBLE COMMENTARY FOR TEACHING AND PREACHING

James Luther Mays, *Series Editor*
Patrick D. Miller, *Old Testament Editor*
Paul J. Achtemeier, *New Testament Editor*

ROBERT W. JENSON

Song of Songs

INTERPRETATION

A Bible Commentary
for Teaching and Preaching

John Knox Press
LOUISVILLE

Scripture quotations from the New Revised Standard Version of the Bible are copyright © 1989 by the Division of Christian Education of the National Council of the Churches of Christ in the U.S.A. and are used by permission.

Library of Congress Cataloging-in-Publication Data

Jenson, Robert W.
    Song of songs / Robert W. Jenson.
        p. cm. — (Interpretation, a Bible commentary for teaching and preaching)
    Includes bibliographical references (p.).
    ISBN 0-8042-3117-6
    1. Bible. O.T. Song of Solomon—Commentaries.   I. Title.   II. Series.

BS1485.53 J46 2005
223'.907—dc22   2005042225

© 2005 Robert W. Jenson
This book is printed on acid-free paper that meets the American National Standards Institute Z39.48 standard. ∞
05 06 07 08 09 10 11 12 13 14 — 10 9 8 7 6 5 4 3 2 1
Printed in the United States of America
John Knox Press
Louisville, Kentucky

SERIES PREFACE

This series of commentaries offers an interpretation of the books of the Bible. It is designed to meet the need of students, teachers, ministers, and priests for a contemporary expository commentary. These volumes will not replace the historical critical commentary or homiletical aids to preaching. The purpose of this series is rather to provide a third kind of resource, a commentary that presents the integrated result of historical and theological work with the biblical text.

An interpretation in the full sense of the term involves a text, an interpreter, and someone for whom the interpretation is made. Here, the text is what stands written in the Bible in its full identity as literature from the time of "the prophets and apostles," the literature that is read to inform, inspire, and guide the life of faith. The interpreters are scholars who seek to create an interpretation that is both faithful to the text and useful to the church. The series is written for those who teach, preach, and study the Bible in the community of faith.

The comment generally takes the form of expository essays. It is planned and written in the light of the needs and questions that arise in the use of the Bible as Holy Scripture. The insights and results of contemporary scholarly research are used for the sake of the exposition. The commentators write as exegetes and theologians. The task they undertake is both to deal with what the texts say and to discern their meaning for faith and life. The exposition is the unified work of one interpreter.

The text on which the comment is based is the Revised Standard Version of the Bible and, since its appearance, the New Revised Standard Version. The general availability of these translations makes the printing of a text in the commentary unnecessary. The commentators have also had other current versions in view as they worked and refer to their readings where it is helpful. The text is divided into sections appropriate to the particular book; comment deals with passages as a whole, rather than proceeding word by word, or verse by verse.

Writers have planned their volumes in light of the requirements set by the exposition of the book assigned to them. Biblical books differ in character, content, and arrangement. They also differ in the way they have been and are used in the liturgy, thought, and devotion of the church. The distinctiveness and use of particular books have been taken into account in decisions about the approach, emphasis, and use of space in the commentaries. The goal has been to allow writers to develop the format that provides for the best presentation of their interpretation.

The result, writers and editors hope, is a commentary that both explains and applies, an interpretation that deals with both the meaning and the significance of biblical texts. Each commentary reflects, of course, the writer's own approach and perception of the church and world. It could and should not be otherwise. Every interpretation of any kind is individual in that sense; it is one reading of the text. But all who work at the interpretation of Scripture in the church need the help and stimulation of a colleague's reading and understanding of the text. If these volumes serve and encourage interpretation in that way, their preparation and publication will realize their purpose.

The Editors

AUTHOR'S PREFACE

The series editors' suggestion that I write the Interpretation commentary on the Song of Songs came as a considerable surprise, since I am a systematic theologian and not a member of the exegetical guild, and since I had for decades turned to Hebrew only to check individual points. "Every systematic theologian," they said, "should write biblical commentary at the end of his career." And that was indeed once the tradition: first systematics, then biblical study. Even Thomas Aquinas's monumental *Summa Theologiae* was intended as mere preparation for meditation on Scripture. So, since the emulation of great examples is a great part of virtue, and since I knew Jim Mays and Pat Miller wished me well, I said I would do it. To be sure, I am not certain how I should take that reference to "the end of his career," or their further suggestion that I was the very one to deal with this particular book.

As I turned to the work, the surprise turned to delight. I have enjoyed few projects so intensely. Both the renewed opportunity for close engagement with a biblical text, and the beauty of this particular text, became something close to obsession. I owe much to Jim Mays and Pat Miller.

The question is of course notorious: Whatever do you do with the Song of Songs, as a biblical text? The interpretive strategy I adopted is described in the introduction; here let me say only that after considering the history of the Song's interpretation I came to it quite quickly, and that I gained confidence as the work proceeded. Whether this lack of struggle is a good sign or a bad one, others must judge. The brief commentary by Ellen Davis and a later article by her were a decisive help in getting me started, though I found I often disagreed with her on particular passages.

I once again thank the Center of Theological Inquiry and its director, Wallace Alston, for my unique position there, into which work on such a project could fit more or less seamlessly. Blanche Jenson is always my chief instigator and critic, but the present case is special. I could not have written a commentary on the Song at all without the experience of our long life together. For the reason of this last, see the citation from Bernard of Clairvaux at the end of the introduction.

Robert W. Jenson
The Feast of Michael and All Angels,
the Year of Our Lord 2004
Princeton, New Jersey

CONTENTS

1:1	INTRODUCTION AND TITLE	1
	Initial Questions	1
	What Plain Sense?	4
	The Overt Sense	8
	Theological Allegory	10
	Human Sexuality as the Analogue	13
	The Plan of the Commentary	14
	Two Final Recommendations	15
1:2–4	Kisses	16
1:5–6	Sun-burned but Beautiful	19
1:7–8	The Shepherdess	23
1:9–17	Mutual Admiration	26
2:1–7	Lovesick and Happy	30
2:8–17	The Voice of the Turtledove	33
3:1–5	Strange Seeking	37
3:6–11	Who Is She?	40
4:1–7	Beauty	44
4:8	From Lebanon	47
4:9—5:1	The Garden	49
5:2–8	Strange Seeking Again	53
5:9–16	His Body	56
6:1–3	The Garden Again	59
6:4–9	A Formidable Woman	62
6:10	Who? Again	65
6:11–12	Amminadib?	68
6:13	The Dancing Shulammite	70
7:1–5	Her Queenly Body	73
7:6–9	The Palm Tree	75
7:10–13	Assignation in the Countryside	79
8	The Last Collection	82
8:1–2	Not Her Brother	83

INTERPRETATION

8:3–4	A Fragment	85
8:5a	Who? Yet Again	86
8:5b–c	Under the Apple Tree	88
8:6–7	The Power of Love	90
8:8–10	The Little Sister Grows Up	95
8:11–12	His Own Vineyard	99
8:13	The Voice of Whom?	101
8:14	Endings	102

BIBLIOGRAPHY 105

Introduction
and Title (1:1)

"Blessed is he who enters holy places, but much more blessed is he who enters 'the Holy of Holies.' . . . Likewise, blessed is he who knows holy songs and sings them . . . , but much more blessed is he who sings 'the Song of Songs'" (Origen, 266).

Initial Questions

The Song of Songs appears in the Christian canon of the Old Testament as the last of five books grouped together as books of "wisdom." But those who read it for a first time, or perhaps for a first time with full attention, may be surprised by what they find, for its overt content is very different from that of the other books of wisdom—or indeed from that of any other book in the Bible. They will find neither ethical-theological reflection as in Job, nor exemplification of that fear of the Lord which is wisdom, as in the Psalms, nor the dicta of sages as in Proverbs or Ecclesiastes—and assuredly not history of salvation or *torah* or prophecy as in the rest of the Old Testament. Instead, they will find explicit, though never quite pornographic, poetry of physical love. Sexual yearning and fulfillment are sung without reticence, moral judgment, or great deference to legal or social constraints. The opening lines set the tone for the whole: without identification or preamble a woman cries, "Let him kiss me with the kisses of his mouth . . . ," and when her lover appears immediately urges haste in moving to a more private chamber. She is, as twelfth-century commentator William of St. Thierry wrote, with a mixture of fascination and alarm, "wholly without modesty" (Norris, 17).

The poetry is in a general sense lyric, presumably intended for some sort of cantillation. It sings the love of a passionate woman and her sometimes elusive and sometimes importunate lover. Most passages tell or suppose some incident in the lovers' affair; some are brief dramatic exchanges. The woman's voice and desires dominate. Besides these two, there are a female chorus and briefly a male chorus or choruses; once or twice the poet may speak in her own voice. Several poems are or include a known Middle Eastern form for which scholarly jargon

1

appropriates an Arabic term: a *wasf* details and praises the person of the beloved. Overtly, the poetry is wholly secular: neither God nor any religious practice or belief is mentioned.

It is therefore not surprising that the Song is one of the three most commented-upon books in the Bible. In the first place, its presence there urgently calls for explanation. Can a canonical book of Scripture really be as secular as this poetry seems to be? In a second place, if it has some hidden religious or theological meaning, how do we discover it? To those who think they know the answer to that last question, the Song then offers unique opportunity for exegetical virtuosity—not to say uncontrolled fantasy.

Yet for all the scholarly and imaginative labor expended over the millennia, there is no long-term consensus in even the most elementary points of the Song's interpretation. The very title can be read differently according to an interpreter's antecedent opinions. For simplicity's sake we will in this commentary continue to call our text simply "the Song."

The usual English translation of the full title is The Song of Songs, Which Is Solomon's (1:1). The first part, "Song of Songs," is the literal translation of a Hebrew phrase that is grammatically clear enough. "F(singular) of F(plural)" is a Hebrew idiom for the superlative, for example, "Lord of Lords" meaning "the most lordly Lord" or "Holy of Holies" meaning "the holiest Holy Place." But then we may observe that this is not a common idiom in the Bible and that most of its other biblical uses are, like these two, somehow related to the superlative being of God (Davis, 240). We may be led to ask: Could someone have intended the construction's theological environment to be noticed? Are we being nudged to think of "The *Godliest* Song"? The earliest surviving scholarly reference to the Song, from around A.D. 100 by the revered Rabbi Aqiba, laid it down that the Song of Songs is the "Holy of Holies" among the holy books of Scripture; perhaps there was some link in tradition between the grammar of his dictum and that of this part of the title—or perhaps there was not.

Then there is the clause "which is Solomon's." This is not necessarily an ascription of authorship, "by Solomon." It could also be rendered "dedicated to Solomon" or "about Solomon" or "in Solomon's style," or perhaps in yet other ways.

Moving on with matters usually covered in the introduction to a biblical commentary, it is a necessary early step in reading any text to get the genre right. If, for example, we read a fictional travel narrative under the impression that it reports an actual journey and try to take the same trip, we court disaster. Unfortunately for those concerned with the Song—whether preachers, teachers, private readers for devotion or pleasure, or writers of commentaries—if we consider the full history of the Song's interpretation and not just the modern period, genre is the chiefly controverted matter. That same first scholarly mention by Rabbi Aqiba was already a polemic against persons who assigned the Song to a different genre than did he—indeed, he consigned them to eternal damnation for profaning so holy a text. Moreover, we will find that interpretation of this text depends even more on the identification of genre than is usually the case.

To be sure, we have already noted some clear points about genre: the Song is lyric love poetry with a continuing cast of personae. But two questions then arise: Is the book simply a collection of poems, or is there some structure of the whole? And above all, who are those lovers? As we shall shortly see, also this second question is a question about genre.

We might expect to get help with both questions—and with the sense of "which is Solomon's"—from the provenance of the poetry, another usual topic in introductions to biblical commentaries. But proposals in this case vary so widely that if we survey them with a minimum of precommitment we must conclude that, pending new discoveries, we can know very little about when—within a span of centuries—where, by whom, or on what occasion or occasions this poetry was written (Murphy, 5).

The Song's great consistency of matter and tone does suggest that one poet or closely knit group of poets is responsible for all or most of it, and this commentary will refer simply to "the poet." Given the viewpoint from which much of the poetry is cast, the poet or a dominating figure among the poets may well have been a woman; our pronoun for the poet will be "she." Past that, there is, in the present commentator's judgment, only one usable lead. Two contemporary commentators of otherwise antithetical views have pointed out a phenomenon insufficiently noted in modern scholarship: the Song is constructed from the language and imagery of the rest of the Old Testament in a fashion unique among the biblical books (LaCocque; Davis). Whoever the poet was otherwise, she was a devotee of the sort of literature that now makes up our Old Testament. We can therefore at least exclude origin outside the culture of Israel—or anyway that part of it represented by the Old Testament—and with it such scholars' fantasies as that the Song was originally a liturgy for the fertility cult of Ishtar and Tammuz, or is an adaptation from the Egyptian.

Moreover, for our poet to have become so steeped in the specific images and language found in the Old Testament canon, many of the documents now in that canon must have been extant and available together in such a way as to speak with one voice; when the Song was

3

written, there must have been a formal or informal library anticipating a canon. Thus very early provenance, certainly Solomon's own time, seems excluded. But these are meager results.

As to a possible overall structure of the Song, agnosticism seems again the wisest course. There have been attempts to construe the Song as a drama, or as a long recitation, perhaps for use at weddings, or as a liturgy (Pope). These have convinced few but their proposers, and all require reconstructive hypotheses supported only by their own internal coherence and the history-of-religions predilections of the proposers. The more modest proposal, that the Song is a structured suite of poems building to an emotional climax, does indeed seem plausible at most points in the Song, but is less easy precisely in the chapter containing the putative climax (8:6–7). The present commentary will therefore adopt another minimal position and take the Song simply as a collection of verses, with consistent personae, a consistent theme and attitude, and some patterns of diction linking groups of poems. Occasionally we will note closer connections between two or three poems in a row. The Song in fact may be more organized, in some way yet to be divined, but we will rely on no supposition about that.

Indeed, of attempts to discover a unifying plot for the Song, the one most influential through history, and one of the most intrinsically interesting, is also one of the least likely. Rabbinic Judaism's exegesis always tended to historicize the Song, to connect events in the lovers' affair with events in Israel's history with the Lord. The Aramaic paraphrase-commentary of the Song, *Targum Canticles*, in its present form probably coming from the seventh century and Palestine (*Targum*, 55–60), took this a step further and found in the Song a complete sequential history of Israel from Abraham to the eschaton. Moreover, according to the *Targum*, the Song portrays a periodic-theological pattern of that history: it presents three cycles of beginning, disaster, and restoration. This reading decisively influenced later Jewish commentary and a minority stream of medieval Christian exegesis. Such interpretation is now likely to be pejoratively labeled "allegorical"; we will come back to that. And we will in the commentary see that on individual passages the *Targum* is well worth citing.

What Plain Sense?

So we have before us a collection of highly sensual love lyrics. It is tempting to leave it at that, as most modern commentators do, even those who then try hard to give the presence of the Song in the canon some theological significance. But rabbinic and churchly scholarship has in any longer run not been able to accept this limit. The Song, after all,

4

is a concern of Christian or Jewish exegesis, and indeed has been preserved at all, only because it is in the Jewish and Christian canons of
Scripture. It need not—as some modern commentators have assumed—
be prudery that moves us to ask what such lyrics are doing there (e.g.,
Pope, 114). All other books of the Old Testament in some way concern
Israel's relation to her God; the supposition is not immediately likely that
a collection of sheerly secular lyrics came among them by pure accident.
The present commentator will claim that the Song indeed provides "a
theology of human sexuality" (Murphy, 101) but *pace* the excellent commentator just cited, the overt sense by itself offers no such thing. Which
brings us to that second question: Who are the lovers?

It was the unanimous answer of Jewish and Christian premodern
exegesis—of the ancient rabbis and the later Jewish commentators, and
of the Fathers of the church and the medieval and Reformation commentators—that these poems belong in the canon because the lovers are
the biblical Lord and his people, whether YHWH and Israel or Christ
and the church, or therein comprised Christ and the believing soul. The
near-unanimous answer of interpreters in the modern period was that
this is "allegorical exegesis" and that such exegesis is a bad thing.

In modern discussions of premodern exegesis, "allegorical" is regularly used imprecisely, and usually pejoratively, for the more correctly
so-called "spiritual" exegesis of the Fathers and medievals, of which allegory was only one mode. The church has read "spiritually" because she
reads the whole of Scripture as a dramatically coherent narrative plot-
ted by the Spirit from creation to consummation, with nonnarrative gen-
res present to point the moral and religious import and context of the
narrative. It was a consequent principle of the church's older exegesis
that in such a dramatically connected narrative all events before the last
are most interesting just as they point forward in the story, which will
usually be perceptible only from the viewpoint of what they point to, and
that one way this happens is that earlier events *figure* later events.

Thus when, for example, Martin Luther in the preface to his translation of the Pentateuch called Aaron a figure of Christ, he did not mean
to deny that there was an Aaron who lived earlier in Israel's history than
Christ, or to say that Aaron's story as a person of that time and place was
unimportant. Quite to the contrary, he meant that in what Aaron did
and suffered, and in how the narrator tells of him, one could see something of why there would be the Christ and so something of what he
would be like, and that in reading passages about Aaron the church
must reckon with this figuration. And, in general, the locus of the
church's spiritual exegesis was in thus reading the Old Testament from
the viewpoint of the New; within this broad sweep of spiritual exegesis,

5

"allegory" was then the most specifically christological of several types. However, to avoid repeated pedantic explanation, this commentary will use the current idiom, and usually speak in its loose general fashion of "allegory."

Allegorical exegesis—also as loosely so called—is thus a churchly exegetical procedure applied principally to narrative texts of the Old Testament. The above paragraphs were needed because for our present task it is vital to be clear: it is one thing to exegete a narrative text allegorically, and a different thing to make the genre judgment that a text presented for interpretation *is itself an allegory*; that is, that its plain sense is precisely its solicitation of realities other than those it overtly mentions—and there are of course many such texts. When the ancient rabbis judged that the Song speaks overtly about two human lovers in order to tell the mutual passion of the Lord and Israel, and when the church's exegetes made a parallel decision, this judgment was not itself allegorical exegesis, in either the current or the more precise use of the term. If the rabbis and the Fathers were right in their judgment about genre, then construing theological allegory for the Song's overtly secular poems is in fact plain-sense reading, and is an allegorizing reading just in the sense that allegory is the sort of interpretation which the text invites the interpreter to employ. In the church's traditional exegesis of the Song, more narrowly named allegorical exegesis then occurred as a second step: when the church read the theological story about the Lord and Israel as a story about Christ and the church. With most of the Song, this step is so short that our commentary will not trouble to announce it, but with a few poems, observation of the step will be important.

Of course the next question is: Were the rabbis and the Fathers right in their assignment of genre? There is again a modern near-consensus: they were not. According to most modern commentators, the poems must have been written as secular love poems and then appropriated for the canon by arbitrarily allegorizing exegesis. We may instance two recent and often helpful commentators who span an ecclesial spectrum: Evangelical (Longman) and Catholic (Bergant). The rabbis, or earlier savants of similar bent, may be thought to have done this on purpose or to have done it unwittingly. They may be supposed to have done it in order to bring the poems into the canon in the first place, or they may be supposed to have found the Song already in the canon and to have made them be allegory to justify their presence after the fact.

The warrants for that "must have been" are, however, surprisingly few and weak—and indeed modernity's dominant position is more often assumed than actually argued. Chief among its warrants is the existence in neighboring ancient cultures of love poetry that the Song strongly

6

resembles and that celebrates love purely between human lovers. The refutation of argument based on this warrant is a simple "So what?" That there is love poetry between creatures scarcely implies there can be no love poetry between Creator and creatures; indeed the contrary inference is the more plausible in the case of Israel's God, who is so deeply involved with his creatures. We may, in fact, speculate further: in Israel's immediate environment there was love poetry between gods and goddesses, which also resembles the secular love poetry; it would have been precisely in line with Israel's general position in that milieu to replace love poetry between deities with love poetry between the one deity and Israel. Finally, the delicately evocative lyricism of the Song would have been the obvious form for a theological poet immersed in the ancient Eastern traditions, as our poet manifestly was—the moderns are indeed right about that.

A second warrant, plainly operative but rarely stated, is the feeling that Israel just could not have produced sexy poetry about the Lord. But since, by the currently dominant account itself, Israel did in fact *read* sexy poetry as poetry about the Lord, this inhibition cannot have been very powerful. Further warrants do not appear.

Therefore a radically dissenting—and only at first glance "conservative"—position is possible, though we will not finally adopt it as a general methodological principle. Since the poet of these songs was a devotedly Scripture-reading Israelite, who cast her lyrics in the language and imagery of that Scripture—that is, of texts which directly tell the Lord's stormy love affair with Israel and sometimes explicitly call it that—there seems to be no reason why such an Israelite poet should not have written these songs for that very love (Davis).

There are other arguments from the text for this view. One poem, which is often regarded as the climax of the Song, 8:6–7, almost compels us to suppose that the poet did intend at least this one of the poems to be about both human lovers with each other and God with Israel; for we will see that in this passage the boundary between a secular reading and a theological reading amounts to no more than the difference between alternative resolutions of a play with mythic names that can hardly be accidental. Further, we will encounter three poems, two of them in a row (5:2–8; 3:1–11), whose overt story is merely bizarre, but which become plausible when construed as invitation to theological allegory. Finally among possible arguments for the poet having set up allegorical reading, it is remarkable that the poems where one of the lovers inventories and praises the other's body, for all the explicit sensuality with which they are invested, stop short at the genitalia or even skip over them; it may be that an Israelite poet, intending the poems to

7

be read about the Lord and Israel, felt that speaking explicitly of penis or vulva smacked just too much of the fertility cults.

Nevertheless, it must be admitted that these considerations are some way from being conclusive, so that agnostic caution will again be the best policy. Fortunately, what we can be certain of is enough to be going on with, if more precariously than we might wish. We do know that so soon as we have any record of the Song's existence, it had its place in the canon, and that the earliest recorded comment on this— Rabbi Aqiba's again—insisted on allegorical-theological identification of the lovers as the reason. In the present commentator's judgment, we can also be certain in dismissing modern exegetes' certainties about the fact or nature of an initial secular life of the Song. Moreover and finally, even if the Song had some precanonical and pretheological existence and even if we knew anything about it, the text as it inhabits the canon is the text for our exegesis. In this case as in others, a reconstructed pre-canonical life of the Song—in this commentator's judgment unachiev-able—could serve only as an aid for the interpretation of the text in its canonical entity.

Perhaps the poems were originally written about the Lord and Israel. Or perhaps they became poems about the Lord and Israel when they were taken into the canon. Or perhaps they came by some now unknowable other route into some precanonical collection and were later made to be poems about the Lord and Israel in order to justify their place in a canon; for exegetical purposes, this possibility anyway collapses into the second. *In whichever of these ways*, the canonical entity is about the love of Israel and the Lord, and to read it by con-struing theological allegory is to read what we may call its canonical plain sense. For what exegetes of other opinion will likely call the "plain" sense, we will speak of the "overt" sense, as in the following.

The Overt Sense

It of course remains that the overt stories and exchanges told or presumed by the poems are enacted between two human lovers, and that our first task must be to offer such clarification of this overt sense as may be in each case needed and possible. We cannot construe alle-gory for a passage until we understand the overt text that solicits it.

In trying to clarify the overt stories we will make what is usually the most natural and is anyway the safest assumption: that the lovers and other personae are fictions interior to a world imagined by a poet, that, for example, the poem alluding to Solomon's wedding day will not be clarified by trying to reconstruct the historical Solomon's—well-used— wedding ritual. In this we depart from the premodern exegetes whose

8

insights we will in other connections seek to reappropriate, for at the level of what the Fathers and others called the "plain narrative" or "historical sense" they of course did not have the heritage of modern historical criticism, and took ascriptions and references to Solomon at historical face value. The third-century Christian polymath Origen of Alexandria set the general pattern for much subsequent premodern Christian exegesis by calling the overt narrative an epithalamium, a "wedding song," in dramatic form, composed by Solomon as if for a royal bride (Origen, 21).

Despite the extreme sensuality of the poems, we will not share some commentators' zeal to discover all possible allusions to genitalia or their uses. Although formal analysis of the Song's prosody—of alliteration, the more subtle parallelisms, and so forth (Bergant)—can be fascinating, this sort of elucidation only once or twice falls within the scope of this commentary. The signs are too plain to be missed, that an editor or editors have at some point shaped the collection as we have it. Beyond this observation, however, little is discernible about this editing, especially about editorial predilections; any attempt at redaction criticism would be mere fantasy.

Following the policy of the series, the text initially taken for comment is the New Revised Standard Version. NRSV usually translates the Hebrew text stabilized by Jewish scholars called "the Masoretes," who worked from the sixth through the tenth centuries. Where the NRSV translators have found the Masoretic text too implausible, and an ancient version—the Syriac, Greek Septuagint, or Latin Vulgate—seems to have translated a more likely Hebrew text, they have sometimes followed the version. In this commentary, we will abide by NRSV where a decision about either text or translation depends mostly on linguistic considerations. Where other than linguistic criteria play a significant role, we will occasionally depart from NRSV, sometimes to what is—remarkably—the one really interesting English alternative, the Authorized or King James Version. We will not make surveys of translations. Following the NRSV in respect for Jewish awe before God's proper name, YHWH will appear in its ancient circumlocution as "the Lord."

It has been this commentator's intent to retrieve insights of Jewish and Christian premodern exegesis, but this is often hindered by the circumstance that for the ancient church the canonical Old Testament was effectively the early Greek translation called the Septuagint—even when the interpreter could read Hebrew—and that later in the West the church's effective Bible was the Latin Vulgate. The difficulty is that in the case of the Song the Septuagint and the Vulgate differ so much from the Masoretic Hebrew that the Fathers' and medievals' comments

9

are often on effectively different—often very different—poems than those before us with NRSV. The problems thereby posed cannot generally be dealt with in this commentary. It is, indeed, a doctrinal question about which the commentator is personally undecided: Is the church's authoritative Old Testament an unavailable "original" Hebrew or the Masoretes' Hebrew or the Septuagint? Also that question cannot be dealt with here.

Translations of citations from Bernard of Clairvaux, Gregory of Nyssa, and Origen are the commentator's. Other citations from the Fathers and Christian medievals are from the translations made by Richard Norris for his anthology of patristic and medieval commentary on the Song.

Theological Allegory

The commentary to follow will be prudent—insofar as that is possible with the Song—and assume only the less radical dissent from current opinion; that is, we will suppose that the canonical Song solicits allegory, but will take no general position about who intended this, the poet or subsequent canonizers. This does make particular exegeses more delicate. If we could be sure that the poet herself intended allegorical reading, we could expect this to show in the texts. And if we look for such signs, and remember that we are dealing with poetry, so that we attend to wordplay, glancing allusions, choices of simile and metaphor, and the like, we do seem to find them. On the supposition that the poet was responsible for such clues—that is to say, that they are indeed "clues"—we could then take them as guides of our reading. Since, however, we will methodologically refrain from that supposition, we cannot proceed so safely.

Since we accept that the rabbinic and patristic genre identification correctly specifies the canonically plain text, are we bound to the rabbis' or the Fathers' specific allegorical readings? Fortunately for our escape from such bondage but unfortunately for the security of our interpretations, there never was a standard rabbinic or churchly allegory for any particular poem. It was taken that the personae of the Song are the Lord and his people, but there was no consensus about what the Song says about them in any individual passage. We are therefore not only free but compelled to find our own best way into each poem.

It may then seem that any and all proposals must be equally appropriate. Texts that provoke allegory but provide no key to the code must obviously be exposed to arbitrary fancy—of which the history of the Song's exegesis provides abundant example. It may seem that everyone can do with the Song as they please—and that therefore, among other

10

things, writing or reading a commentary is superfluous. And, indeed, proposals of the Song's theological allegory will inevitably be somewhat individual; one reader may perceive one theological story and another a different one. This does not, however, mean that all proposals are equal; there are some controls.

If we had access to the intent of the author, we could control our discernment of theological allegory by that intent and so by actual clues left by the author. We have decided not generally to rely on this assumption. Even so, with individual images or phrases it sometimes does seem that the text itself is prodding us to a theological reading; we are sometimes compelled to think, "The poet can hardly have written '. . .' without expecting hearers or readers to think of . . . ."

Of the intent of whoever definitively made Scripture of the Song, we can be more certain: they intended the Song to be about Israel and the Lord. Yet even here, as we have noted, there is no consensus about what individual passages say about Israel and the Lord.

What can and must chiefly discipline our theological-allegorical proposals, is what we may call the *canon's* own intent for the Song. That is, our discernments of a theological story for the overt story are—precisely historically!—appropriate if they fit the text's overt story and if they draw from, and are in accord with, the account of the Lord and his people told by the whole of Scripture. Moreover, that the Song is in the Jewish and Christian canons sets the community of interpretation. We should read as if we were reciting in synagogue or at Eucharist, and only within the structure and rhetoric of such events let the Song's apparent allusions play out.

Nor can or should we simply leap over the hermeneutical history between us and the older interpreters. Inevitably and rightly, beneficiaries of modernity's "historical-critical" attitude, even when interpreting lyrics that invite allegory, and the imagination appropriate to the genre, will often perceive different lines of allusion than did the older interpreters, and what we will judge a plausible proposal of theological story will often be commended by different criteria than theirs. It was of course just such modern intuitions that occasioned rejection above of the *Targum's* overall construal.

Several considerations may be adduced under this last general rubric. For one, modernity's acute awareness of genre will prohibit proposals of allegory that do not reckon with these texts' obvious character as lyric poetry. A great deal of premodern interpretation must by this criterion appear as simply inadmissible. And indeed, when we turn to 11 the new and excellent anthology of patristic and medieval exegesis (Norris), or to the premodern Christian commentaries more directly mined for this commentary, we find much brilliant theology and profound spirituality, but a disappointing harvest of allegory plausibly solicited by the particular text under consideration rather than by any other.

Second, the poems, at the immediately observed level that modernity is always and rightly careful to honor, are *erotic love* poetry. If they are about the Lord and his people, it is the erotic love between the Lord and his people that we have to expound, not, for example, the disembodying of the soul in prayer or the proper care of talmudic students—neither of which examples is made up. And third, an observable affinity with the literature of Wisdom, reflected in the Christian ordering of the Old Testament, generally inhibits finding narrative of actual sequences of saving history. Like Wisdom, the Song is about what is foundationally the case between God and his people; thus in the instances where the solicited theological story tells a sequence of saving events, it is the exodus itself that is told.

Readers will undoubtedly sometimes decide that the commentary's proposal of a theological story is unconvincing. Given the character of our text, they can without sarcasm be invited to do better. It may be that the chief purpose of a commentary on this text is not to provide interpretation but to provoke it.

Finally, the real control of our reading is not one we can wield. The sundry books of the Bible are *Scripture*, a tool of the Spirit to guide the church, in that the Spirit guides also the church's exegesis. The Fathers therefore unanimously maintained that the chief thing we could do to seek right interpretation of Scripture—and especially of Scripture that like the Song solicits active imagination—was to pray for the Spirit's control. They were right.

To conclude this section, we may ask what the Song's theological allegories—or anyway those proposed in the following—contribute to our biblical-theological understanding. In fact, the allegories that we will discern for the Song amount to an entire theology, with two special features. First, it is neither narrative nor didactic, but lyrical, theology intended to be perceived obliquely and savored for its images and allusions; the beauty of these poems is part of their theological meaning. Second, it portrays the love between the Lord and his people as *desire*. With his immensely influential *Agape and Eros*, Anders Nygren persuaded three generations of theologians and exegetes that self-giving love, *agape*, and desire, *eros*, are two incompatible sorts of love, and that only the former characterizes the relation between the biblical God and his people; no allegory plausibly solicited by the Song can agree.

Human Sexuality as the Analogue

There is a final and decisive methodological point to be made. We will read the Song as a solicitation of theological allegory. And we will suppose that in so doing we find truth. That is, we will suppose that the Song's canonical plain sense *rightly* takes human sexual love as an analogue of the love between the Lord and Israel. But right analogies between divine and human characters or acts work both ways: they enable and structure human speech about God, and they just so show us the truth of the human matters invoked to do this. In the present instance, if human sexuality can be an analogue of divine-human love, it must somehow be correlate to, or able to be correlate to, that love. It is a principle of classical theology: in this life we cannot know what it is like to be God—in the traditional language, we cannot know his "essence"—and nor then what it is like to love as God loves. Thus we do not know *how* our penultimate human love is like God's. But we can know *that* it is, and thereby know truth also about our loves.

The old churchly exegetes, having discerned a theological story for the overt story, regularly stopped there. They indeed understood the two-sidedness of analogy; thus the same William of St. Thierry wrote: "[T]hough a person . . . is spiritual, nevertheless the pleasures of the flesh are natural to him . . . ; and once they have been taken captive by the Holy Spirit, he embraces them as part of his allegiance to spiritual love" (Norris, 17). But they do not develop what this embrace might mean for the practice of the flesh's pleasures.

There is a regrettable theological reason for this. The Fathers performed a marvel in bending the suppositions and language of the Greek thinkers, that is, of their own native world of thought, to the gospel's purposes, but at a few points the adapted notions remained unbaptized. One such point was that soul and body continued in some contexts to be conceived not merely as different but as antithetical. So the great Gregory of Nyssa in the fourth century: "What has the immaterial . . . soul to do with material things . . . ? That inner fount of knowledge must not waste itself on what is foreign to it—that is, on bodily matters" (Gregory, 9, 277). Thus for the Fathers and medievals, once the reader has made the ascent to a spiritual reading, to go back and consider bodily matters would be a relapse.

Thereby the older exegesis indeed did the Song violence; there is a vital moment of truth in modernity's rebellion against it. For the poems remain, whosoever affair they narrate, sensual love poetry. They are about erogenous zones and seductive aromas and lovers looking for a place to be alone and frustration and the morning after.

13

Whether the poet intended it or canonization imposes it, the Song's canonical entity posits an analogy of the love between human lovers with the relation between God and his people, precisely with respect to the erotic aspect of human love. By the classic understanding of Creator/creature analogies, most clearly developed by Thomas Aquinas, this does not mean that our eroticism is the original and that we construe God's relation to his people by projecting it—as recent "metaphor theology" rather naively supposed. Just the other way around, it means that human lovers' relations to each other are recognizable in their true eroticism only by noting their analogy to an eroticism that is God's alone. Just as in general our faulty righteousness can nonetheless be anticipation of our eschatological sharing in God's own righteousness, only so to be righteousness at all, so our frail eroticism can be an anticipation of final sharing in the fulfillment of God's and his people's desire for one another.

Also under this heading, we may ask: What is the Song's contribution within the whole of Scripture? The answer this time is very simple: if the considerations just adduced are correct, then the Song, after its way through theological allegory, provides the chief biblical resource for a believing understanding of human sexuality, of the *lived meaning* of "Male and female he created them."

The Plan of the Commentary

The commentary will not be organized by verse or chapter, but by poem. The units we will treat as individual poems are often shorter than those proposed by other commentators, who sometimes perceive more continuity between verses than the present commentator is able to do.

For each poem we will follow a three-step pattern of interpretation, in accord with the analysis above. A first section will offer such explanation of the overt story as seems needed and possible. A second section will propose theological allegory. So far we will have followed Gregory of Nyssa's methodological mandate: "We must first draw out the sense present in the lines as they stand, and then connect these inspired words to what is to be envisioned" (Gregory, 6, 173). And a third will consider what may be said about our created sexuality in view of the divine-human analogies exploited by the poem under consideration.

Both the total space devoted to a poem and the balance of space devoted to the three sections will vary considerably from poem to poem. It will not always be convenient to keep the three discussions neatly separate, though we will maintain the distinct sections. Comment on the first two poems will be oversized, since they provide opportunity to discuss certain matters of general application without further distending this introduction by taking them up here; readers may wish

14

to read these before turning to other passages of their interest. A general comment on the state of chapter 8 will be intruded before the commentaries on individual units.

Citations from premodern Christian exegesis will pile up with earlier poems and become scarce with later ones, since the three generally thought most important, and most drawn on here, are all incomplete. Gregory of Nyssa and Bernard of Clairvaux never finished their expositions, and the last two thirds of Origen's foundational works are lost.

Where references in parentheses appear with the author or editor's name only, they are either general or at the place. As is usual with ancient texts, Gregory of Nyssa and Bernard of Clairvaux are cited by standard internal numbering systems, to allow use of various editions. No useful system of this sort is provided for Origen on the Song; he will therefore be cited by page in Lawson's translation.

The character of the Song, as a set of love lyrics with most of the same personae from one lyric to another, with the same erotic intensity, and with no certain dramatic or conceptual progression of the whole, compels the commentator to say the same thing about passage after passage. And the location of the most theologically packed poem (8:6–7) only at the very end of the book compels postponement of central matters. Readers should not expect a conceptually sequential exposition.

Two Final Recommendations

Do not read the commentary on any poem before you have read the poem itself, more than once and preferably aloud. And should you wish to join the *church's* long engagement with the Song, let all be done with prayer for the love the Song praises. Bernard of Clairvaux wrote: in this book "it is everywhere love that speaks. If anyone hopes to grasp the sense of what he reads, let him love. Whereas someone who does not love will hear or read this song of love in vain" (Bernard, 79, 1).

1:2–4
Kisses

I

The Song does not open with abstract praise of love, or with love of a sublimated sort, but with a demand for kisses, and apparently with haste for something more than kisses. Both are solicited by a woman whose cry is her only introduction, and who will be the dominant and more eager persona through most of the Song. She will have no name until 6:13, supposing that "the Shulammite" is a name and that the Shulammite is indeed the same woman as the persona of the other poems.

Verses 2–4b are the woman's voice, and verses 4c–f the voice of a female chorus who will appear in several of the poems. The woman's shifts between third person and second person reference to her lover are initially disconcerting, but we should probably think of verses 2–3 as soliloquy spoken in the physical absence of the lover, and so as encompassing both absence and imagined presence—in any case, such shifts may be a convention of an ancient Middle Eastern genre of love poetry (Murphy). On this supposition, the lover enters with verse 4.

Some commentators think that the Song's lovers do not consummate their love in this poem, and even propose this as a moral lesson. But the woman's haste and their remembered and/or anticipated entry—the time sequences are not clear—into an inner chamber surely suggest at least progress in that direction. That the lover is kingly we will within the overt story regard merely as a standard trope of love poetry. There are others who love him, and we are told that they are right to do so, that he is in fact adorable.

II

Thus when we read the Song for the love between Israel and the Lord, its account of that love does not begin with the Lord's initiative, but with Israel's longing and the Lord's desirability. Such theology is in the tradition founded by St. Augustine: as the famous line from his *Confessions* has it, "You have made us for yourself, and our hearts are restless till they find their rest in you." If it is grace that enables and impels the longing, this grace is not, as in the narrative or prophetic parts of Scripture, a specific historical act of God, but appears throughout the Song, as in the books of Wisdom, rather as an atmosphere in which the

16

personae move. And if we must indeed distinguish between *agape*, self-giving love, and *eros*, desire, allegory solicited by the Song does not suppose that *agape* is the only sanctioned love between God and his people. In this poem, Israel *desires* the Lord, her love is precisely erotic; and later in the Song we will see that the Lord desires Israel.

Our poem's soteriology is thus that of the church fathers, especially those in the East—and indeed exposition of the Song was a favorite way for them to describe salvation. Israel does not here long for forgiveness of sin or rescue from disaster or for other gifts detachable from the Giver, as Western theology tends to conceive salvation, but simply for the Lord *himself*. Moreover, the longing is aesthetic rather than ethical; it is longing for the Lord's touch and kiss and fragrance. The Lord is simply lovable, and salvation is union with him, a union for which sexual union provides an analogy.

Insofar as God is Israel's object and yearning is the relation, the poem's sense for reality may be called eschatological. The eschatology is both realized and futurist: the king has already brought Israel into his chamber, yet in the present she again yearns for him.

In the present tense we hear of anointing oils, of an inner chamber, and of "the king." No doubt these are in the overt story literary devices internal to the tale of human lovers: every lover is a king and every beloved a princess; the connection between scents and lovemaking is as contemporary as it is ancient; and a next step past kisses may well seek a more private room. But hearers and readers of the sort anticipated by the poet or canonizers, steeped in biblical language, can hardly hear of "the king" without some thought of the Lord; it was after all said that "kingship belongs to the LORD" (Ps. 22:28). Given the anointing oils, we may even catch a hint of the Messiah, of *the* King of Israel. And are we to hear of inner chambers for union between God and creature without thinking of the Temple's innermost chamber, where Israel and the Lord embrace?

The rabbis, bereft of the Temple by its second and apparently final destruction in A.D. 70, interpreted the kisses of Israel and the Lord as the giving of the Law at Sinai, when the Lord "spoke with us face to face" (*Targum*). For *torah*, unlike even an intact Temple, can be taken into all the places of Israel's exile and dispersion. *Canticles Rabbah* has it: "The commandment itself went in turn to each of the Israelites and said to him, 'Do you undertake to keep me . . . ?' [He] would reply, 'Yes, Yes,' and straightaway the commandment kisses him on the mouth" (*Targum*).

Here we may pause to amplify a general point about interpreting the Song, both the overt story and the theological story. We must always remember that the Song, whoever may be the lovers, is lyric verse. Poets and literary theorists rightly warn that to interpret lyric poetry by saying

17

in prose what the poem and its bits "mean" is to violate it, perhaps fatally. Indeed, it is perhaps best to interpret lyrics only by the verbal recitation for which they are written; but since author and readers of this volume are already several pages into a prose commentary, it is too late for us to be so prudent. If there is then to be prose interpretation and if it is not to fight with its matter, we must at least allow for the evanescent and indirect reference by which lyric verse inhabits reality. The prose mind may well ask, for example, Is the poem's inner room "really" the Holy of Holies, even allegorically? But how would one answer that question? There are methods to determine the lexicography of the Hebrew word used in the passage. But what methods are available to make the poem's reference univocal? Or if "the king" makes us think of the Messiah, then it does.

Christian interpretation of this passage should aim above all so to limn the beauty of God as to make hearers long for his presence. It should proclaim the Johannine Christ, the Revealer of God's glory. It should inspire the hope for union with God that is this Gospel's promise. And it should itself enact present divine beauty, in the beauty of its own rhetoric and use of Scripture. For help in understanding all this, a preacher or teacher might well turn to Jonathan Edwards, who in his *Personal Narrative* wrote of his conversion, "I remember the thought I used then to have of holiness. . . . It appeared to me that there was nothing in it but what was ravishingly lovely," and whose whole theology is one vast development of that vision—on account of which he will appear several times in this commentary.

Indeed, a public use of this passage should make hearers long even to *touch* God. And it should remember that the biblical God has made provision for that very thing also: for our lips to touch his body and for us to savor the wine of that kiss. Bernard of Clairvaux, with most of the Christian tradition, read the woman as simultaneously the church and the believing soul, and the lover as Christ. With both the scene of Luke 7:36–50 and the Eucharist in mind, he wrote: "'I cannot be at peace,' she says, 'unless he kisses me with the kiss of his mouth. I give thanks for the kiss of his feet, and for the kiss of his hand; but if he cares for me at all, let him kiss me with the kiss of his mouth. I am not ungrateful, but I love. I have received more than I deserve . . . , but less than I want. Desire moves me, not reason. Modesty indeed protests, but love conquers'" (Bernard, 9, 2). And Origen, thinking of the revelation in Christ, has the people of God petition the Father for Incarnation: "[M]oved by pity for my love, send him, that he may no longer speak to me through his ministering angels and prophets only, but may come in person, and 'kiss me with the kisses of his mouth,' that is, pour his words from his mouth into mine" (Origen, 60).

18

III

Our poem speaks of a love that occurs as sweet bodily kisses, and of desperate need for such love; and its allegory uses both as an image of the relation between the Lord and his people. What does the possibility of this use tell us about the image itself?

If bodily love can be an appointed image of union with God, then we may not suppose that love becomes purer or nobler by disembodiment. If there is such a thing as love that needs no touching, it is not this love that in the Song mirrors the love between Israel's God and his people, whatever may be true of the gods of the religions or the philosophers.

During the recent sexual "revolution" those among the mass fornicators who still felt that their practices needed justification sometimes said, "It's only bodies, after all"; and of course philandering men have long argued, "It didn't mean anything." Precisely such opinion is the most precise self-manifestation of the evil that currently infests us. It is the very kissing or what it leads to—or in the other direction at various diminutions, the touch on the shoulder or the look in the eye or the voice-sound on the telephone—that is analogous to union with God. This is even true negatively of faithless or corrupt touching, as Paul pointed out (1 Cor. 6:15–20).

Nor in the Song's ethics is neediness a bad thing. If Israel can be said to need the Lord and if the Lord accepts such desire, then need for the other must be a good. Through the modern period, personal need has been taken as weakness, and women's supposed greater neediness—which indeed seems to appear in the Song—as a mark of their inferiority. Late modernity even came to regard needing the other as actual vice; a few years before this writing, the happily married were told they should find some occasion of conflict, as antidote for their "codependence." The Song knows better: we were made for, and therefore need not only God but the created other, in whom the heart may find some rest also penultimately to union with God.

1:5–6
Sun-burned but Beautiful

I

The whole of this piece is in the voice of the woman, addressing the chorus. These are now identified as women of Jerusalem, which in context seems to mean upper-class city women.

The overt story perhaps needs some explanation. The similes presume an ethnic group with a complexion not immune to visible tanning. And unlike the late-modern West, most such societies have regarded a woman's tan as a mark of low social status: tan betrays her as a peasant who must work out of doors instead of staying indoors guarding her complexion. The Jerusalem women stare at the woman of the Song because she is deeply tanned, and she defends herself. She says that her brothers—who in Mideastern societies disciplined their sisters—have for some reason punished her with work in the family vineyard; her tan is thus the mark of a particular delinquency and not of status. Moreover, she defies the status standard of beauty altogether, by proclaiming that this punishment does not diminish her beauty; on the contrary, she is beautiful just because she is tanned; her punishment has beautified her.

The similes by which the woman praises her tan may be puzzling: her darkness is like that of the tents of the nomadic tribe "Kedar"—if that is indeed how we are to understand "tents of Kedar"—or like "the curtains of Solomon." A first puzzlement is the nature of the similes: most women would not now boast that their complexion resembled goat-hair canvas or untanned animal skin, the materials of ancient desert tents.

Here can be occasion for comment on a general character of the Song's similes and metaphors: as elsewhere in ancient poesy, the point or points of comparison are sometimes very limited and not located where moderns may expect them to be. In our poem, the similes put her darkness, which the chorus takes as a mark of the woman's low status, in correspondence with the visually dark tents of a tribe noted for its power and with the in some way dark "curtains" of no less glorious a personage than Solomon. No more is done or needed. My tan, says the woman by her similes, raises rather than lowers my status. *Why* her darkness assimilates her to power and glory is unsaid in the overt story.

One simile poses a material question also; and its likely answer is a lead to a theological story. What are "the curtains of Solomon"? A reader or listener—modern or ancient—whose imagination is stocked from Scripture must surely think of hangings in Solomon's Temple. Indeed, the word used here is the same as that used in Exodus for the hangings that made up the wilderness tabernacle, which was thought to have been the Temple's pattern. Thus there is also a parallel between the Temple or tabernacle, the latter a nomadic tent-sanctuary, with the tents of the nomadic or seminomadic Kedar. And the tabernacle's or Temple's hangings may well be associated with a darkness, though of a different sort than that made by dyes. Such references noted, we may also glimpse a reason for the woman's pride in her tan.

Then at the end, the woman's speech veers from simile into metaphor. The woman has her own vineyard, which she has not cared for. This vineyard cannot be a patch of ground planted to grapes, like that in which she was put to labor; a woman of the ancient Middle East still dependent in her parental house could not own such a thing. Given sexual associations made throughout the Song, we can hardly read the line otherwise than as musing confession of failure to guard her body. Perhaps this is what the brothers punished her for.

II

It is a refrain of the prophets: Israel has not guarded her vineyard. It is another refrain of the prophets: when Israel's infidelities become intolerable, she is punished. She is exiled to strange labor and is deprived of the worship in ornament and song that should make her beautiful in the eyes of the Lord. Just at this point, however, the Israel of our poem surprisingly rejoices; this very punishment beautifies and elevates her. The theology of this bit of allegory is easily ascertained and quickly stated, but is inexhaustible in its depth: the punishments that Israel or the church brings upon herself, and by which she becomes ugly in the eyes of the world, are the very means by which the Lord glorifies her.

According to John's Gospel, it is precisely the cross of Christ that is his elevation to supreme status; and Paul glories only in his weakness. All Christian mystics have reported: the darkness is the light. Those willing to sample where such reflections can take us, might ponder the famous nineteenth and twentieth of Martin Luther's *Heidelberg Theses*: "He is not properly called a theologian who beholds the invisible things of God, known in the creatures; he is properly called a theologian who knows the visible and indecent parts of God, beheld in sufferings and the cross." One may even think of the notorious exclamation of Easter Eve's liturgy: "Oh *fortunate sin* [of Adam and Eve], that occasioned so great a redemption!" And Bernard of Clairvaux wrote of the church and/or the believing soul: "At once tent of Kedar and sanctuary of God! At once earthly dwelling and heavenly palace . . . ! At once a body of death and a temple of light! At once despicable to the proud and the Bride of Christ!" (Bernard, 27, 14).

As to how it can happen that the ugly sinner is beautiful, Gregory of Nyssa commented, "When [the Lord] takes some black soul to himself, he makes it beautiful by communion with himself" (Gregory, 49). If we ask where this marvelous exchange takes place, the similes will not let us forget the Temple. There the curtained Most Holy Place is

21

where in vision the Lord may be seen high and lifted up (Isa. 6). And at the end of these associations, Christians may remember the Lord's promise: his body, the church, will be their temple (John 2:19–22).

The *Targum* paraphrases verse 5: "When the people of the House of Israel made the Calf, their faces became as dark as the sons of Cush who dwell in the tents of Kedar, but when they returned in repentance and were forgiven, the radiance of the glory of their faces became as great as the angels, because they had made curtains for the Tabernacle, and the *Shekhinah* had taken up its abode among them" (*Targum*).

III

What then, the other way around of the analogy, are we to think about comeliness in this world? That it is connected to status, as in the overt story of our poem, is undeniable, in both directions: what the world calls beautiful is at least in part determined by class, and just so, what one cultivates as beauty shows one's class. In some tribal societies, what moderns call obesity has been a chief aspect of beauty, as it shows ability to obtain rich food. "Black is beautiful" could only be proclaimed as African Americans broke down their segregation as an oppressed class; before then relatively light skin counted as more beautiful also among them.

In the theological story for this passage, these connections remain, but subject to the rule that the first shall be last and the last shall be first. Something of that reversal must afflict believers' earthly beauties also.

That is not to say that beauty is a negligible matter; also the Israel of our allegory remains concerned about her appearance before the Lord. But she defies the world's judgment of it. What Israel finally knows as beauty the world does not, and this must warn us also in the matter of our penultimate beauties of face, and of body and dress. Even in this realm, the world's judgments must not rule: for relatively trivial example, the models for advertising display of upscale clothing are now usually chosen for a sullen and abandoned appearance, neither of which can be beautiful in the eyes of faith.

The woman's lover does not appear in this poem, but surely it is he for whom she knows she is beautiful; the Lord sees Israel's beauty also in her deprivations. Thus our poem teaches lovers: gaze also on what in others' eyes would be the beloved's deficiencies, on the "sunburn," his incipient potbelly or her too short nose. They are not there to put us off, but to be transformed by the grace of affection into occasions of endearment—which of course is not to say that help in reducing the potbelly would not be an appropriately loving gesture.

22

And what are we to think of the far more decisive matter of infidelity and forgiveness? When the loved one has not guarded the vineyard of his or her body? In the allegory, punishment and forgiveness are simultaneous, indeed, are but two sides of one divine act of redemption. Can or should it work that way between human lovers?

Since the betrayed human lover is not God, he or she cannot fully transcend the difference between punishment and forgiveness. Nor does a human lover have the right or calling to punish, except in a last extremity that imposes action to separate entirely. But the betrayed lover ineluctably must relate differently to the betrayer, which will be a punishment even when not intended as such. In the suffering and labor of both forgiving the betrayer and willy-nilly punishing him or her, the divine simultaneity of forgiveness and punishment will not be achieved, but it can and should appear as a regulating vision. With us, punishment and forgiveness will remain two different things, but the back and forth between them can converge on that perfection to which we will be admitted as children of our heavenly Father, who is perfect.

1:7–8
The Shepherdess

I

Undeniably, there is about this scene something of Marie Antoinette playing shepherdess in her play farm at Versailles. The goats in this poem are not themselves metaphor but together with the woman are internal to one side of the metaphor; they are in relation to her to be taken as real goats that she tends. And one just does not believe the "most beautiful among women" tending such a flock except in play— not if you have ever encountered a flock of the white angora-type goats envisaged in the Song, from the distance a beautiful sight apt for metaphor and simile, but quite something else at shepherding distance. Nor is there here any suggestion of punishment, as in an earlier poem. And of course the fictive shepherd and shepherdess are a common trope in the romances of many cultures.

The pastoral fiction itself is mostly clear enough. The woman seeks an idyll with her lover, and he is coy: "Follow the other shepherds" is not very forthcoming. One point is obscure, and likely to remain so. The woman needs directions lest she be like someone or something undesirable. But what the Hebrew text intends that to be, we can only guess:

23

NRSV's translation, "one who is veiled," is conjecture, as are commentators' explanations of why that would be bad. The alternatives proposed in translations other than NRSV—for example, AV's more literal "one that turneth aside"—are even less illuminating.

II

Is there any basis for spinning a theological story for this conventionally romantic scene? The rabbis and the Fathers do not offer reassuring precedents, proposing allegory that cannot but appear preposterous to even the most chastened modern sensibility—and let it be said here once for all that this is often the case. Thus the *Targum* exactly reverses the woman's desire to avoid other flocks into a command from God that she resist her inclination to mingle with them, and it makes the flocks that Israel is to avoid be Christianity and Islam, her "kids" young talmudic students, and the tents to which she is to bring them the *shul* (*Targum*). Augustine has a remarkably similar reading: the marriage between Christ and the church is endangered by other flocks, who turn out to be Augustine's usual opponents in his diocese (Norris).

Yet a theological story surely lies very close at hand. That Israel or the church or individual believers are to seek the Lord is a truth of both testaments in both communities. And it is a fact of all Jewish and Christian experience, also as recorded in Scripture, that the Lord's directions for finding him are often far from straightforward or helpful—they are often, as Isaiah and Paul agree, past finding out. What, for example, were Jews of Jeremiah's time, learned in existing Scripture, to make of Jeremiah's alleged word from the Lord that they were now to seek the Lord in Babylon, the very prototype of distance from him (Jer. 29:7)? How exactly was that to be done? As for Christians, it is all very well to try to obey the command to come with other believers to where, in the formula of the Augsburg Confession, "the gospel is rightly preached and the sacraments ministered in accord therewith." But then one must find someplace where this regularly happens. We have to hope that the Lord is indeed sometimes coy with us, for alternative diagnoses of the presenting conditions are even more alarming.

Preaching or teaching of this text will have to summon the courage to abandon justifications of God's ways, to give up solutions to the so-called problem of theodicy. It is a predilection of the present commentator to quote Martin Luther on such matters. On the present topic, Luther's mature judgment, in his treatise on *The Bondage of the Will*, was that if we consider the observable ways in which God rules his cre-

24

ation, and judge by any standard available to us, we must conclude that "either God is malicious or does not exist." Or we may consider Ivan Karamazov's verdict in Dostoyevsky's *The Brothers Karamazov*, that he does not necessarily believe there is no God, but declines to have anything to do with a God who would allow the gratuitous torture of even one child. Jewish or Christian theology that merely turns aside from such judgments forfeits all claim to be taken seriously, at least so immediately after the twentieth and bloodiest of centuries. Faith in God's goodness is always a great and liberating "nevertheless . . . ," and particularly so at this juncture of history.

It will often be so: we will inquire of the Lord, "Tell us, you whom my soul loves, where may I find you?" And the Lord will answer, "If you do not already know, ask around."

III

Should penultimate lovers play with each other in the fashion of this shepherd and shepherdess? Only, one may think, if they are very sure of one another—as the Lord and his people may be, despite everything adduced in the previous paragraphs. With sufficient mutual faithfulness, teasing can be good.

So far so cheerful. But we must also consider how quickly charmed recognition of God's teasing can turn into unbelief in his justice. Of this too our penultimate loves are an analogue. Can we always be transparently fair with one another? Surely not. If we must sometimes defy Ivan Karamazov to cling to a God whose justice remains opaque, we must sometimes hold to one another in much the same way. Matters will not come out evenly between lovers, and the more justified I think the grievance is that I nurse against my beloved, the more destructive my brooding must be. "Do not let the sun go down on your anger," with or without arriving at justice, is indeed the mandatory policy centuries of wise folk have called it.

Moreover, the connection between the theological story and its created analogue is in this case causal: if with Ivan we demand that God be fair, we must eventually turn from him; and if we turn from God, we will soon turn from one another also. Despite the best efforts of secularist moralists, Ivan's creator is regularly proved right: if there is no God, then all is permitted. The first place where this will and does now appear is in the closest analogy to our relation to God, our sexual lives.

The Lord and Israel could love one another despite the Lord's coyness—and, of course, Israel's unfaithfulness—because they were bound by the covenant. Contrary to what many ideologists assume, the evidence

25

is that when spouses were legally bound to one another, there was more loving passion in the world—even fornication and adultery had more significance. At least in the church and in marriage that she blesses, the bond can—and perhaps more to the present point—must hold.

1:9–17
Mutual Admiration

I

We will take verses 9–17 together as one long poem, though some commentators read them as separate three-verse poems. The verses are strings of compliments, and can be so easily read as an exchange between the man and the woman that we probably should do so. Some of the lovers' mutual praises require little explanation; one is, to say the least, arresting; and some so strongly suggest an exchange of compliments also between the Lord and his beloved people that it is hard to think the suggestion is not intended by the poet.

This time the man leads, and with an alarming simile. Two explanations vie in the modern literature. Some scholars reach to show that direct comparisons between a woman's beauty and that of a mare were not unknown in ancient poetry. There are two difficulties with this: they have to reach quite far indeed; and the Egyptians seem never to have used mares with their chariots, a circumstance that even the peculiarities of ancient lyric simile will hardly accommodate. Others advert to an anciently proverbial incident when an opposing general let a mare in heat loose athwart the charge of the Pharaoh's stallion-pulled chariots. Should the latter be the simile—as we will in the following suppose it must be—we now know how the woman initially affected her lover: he took one look and was off. The praise of the woman's jewels and the promise to provide more are, of course, intended to redound on their wearer: "My dear, how beautiful you look in them!"

Verses 12–14 are then in the woman's voice. The proposed translations of verse 12 are guesses; the Hebrew for which NRSV proposes "couch" and AV "table," would be literally translated "surrounding place." Plainly, we cannot reliably translate verse 12, and therefore do not know what occasions the effusion of the woman's nard. In any case, the woman 26 continues on the theme of love and scent: from the lover's lodgment between her breasts, he is as fragrant to her as are myrrh and henna, or perhaps is himself anointed with them. In verse 15 the man returns with a simile less alarming than his first; here the point of comparison need be nothing more than the beauty and supposed gentleness of doves, though some have pointed to the dove-shaped eyes of Egyptian female statues.

As the man praised the woman by way of her jewelry, so in verses 16–17 the woman praises him by way of the place of their love-making. Her metaphors seem mixed: in one line they are out in the greenery, in the next in a chamber of precious and—again!—aromatic woods.

II

The woman's metaphors are mixed—unless the place of the love-making is the Temple, built indeed with cedar and other exotic woods of Lebanon, and decorated as a garden. The *Targum's* riff on verse 7 is remarkable: "Solomon the prophet said: 'How fair is the Temple of the Lord that has been built from cedar-wood, but fairer still will be the Temple that will be built in the days of the King Messiah, the beams of which will be of cedars from the Garden of Eden, and its joists will be of cypress, teak and cedar'" (*Targum*).

The question allegorically posed by the opening simile is: Why did the Lord choose Israel? The simile concurs with the theology of Deuteronomy and the general "Deuteronomistic" editing of the Pentateuch, which insists that it was not because Israel was such a prize among the nations that the Lord made her his own, but because he loved her, a reason behind which Deuteronomy forbids us to penetrate. The Lord's election of this people was neither a rational decision nor an arbitrary one; it was of another sort altogether: he loved her. She was beautiful in his eyes, and like the man in the overt story, who was so immediately struck with *eros* that he dares the simile of the mare, he wanted her. Notoriously, such choices need no other reasons than themselves. Bernard of Clairvaux knew what love is: "Love suffices for itself. . . . It loves what it loves, and nothing else moves it. . . . I love because I love; I love in order to love" (Bernard, 83, 3–4). While this may often be a problematic aspect of love among us, it could not be otherwise with God, who, as Karl Barth developed in detail and great depth, *is* his own decision, so as to need or abide no external reasons for his choices.

Two further points must be noted about our poem's evocation of God's love for Israel and her return of it. First, its intensely sensual atmosphere. We are again warned away from either spiritualizing or moralizing the Lord's covenant with Israel. The Lord and Israel, Christ and the church, want each other, and each rejoices in every aspect of the other's beauty. One may even suggest that, like the man in the overt

27

story, God rejoices in the jewelry—of vessels and stained glass and mosaic and weaving and fresco and . . .—with which the church sometimes decks herself when she approaches him. Second, again there is a suggestion of the Temple as the place of their passionate union; and following the Temple's destruction this may well be extended to the portable temples of Christ's eucharistic body or the Torah scroll.

Moreover, preaching or teaching led by the allegory to which this poem invites cannot avoid some hard truths that contemporary Christianity likes to overlook. The Bible's God is sheer contingency: he is the one who chooses what he chooses because he chooses it; he is the one who is what he is because he is it; and for whom this coincidence of fact and reason is not necessity but freedom. In consequence, his relation to Israel and the church can only be truly described with such alarming concepts as election or predestination—or love. The classic evocations of how that works are Paul's letter to the Galatians for the church and Augustine's *Confessions* for individuals.

Just so, the Lord's choice of his people should call forth that people's praise with the most vivid poetic vocabulary of which they are capable—or of which they are not yet capable. It is surely not too immediate a reference to present problems to note that the ditties so beloved of "contemporary worship" do not quite measure up to, for example, "The Lord is unto me as a cluster of camphire in the vineyards of Engedi"—from AV's rendering of verse 14.

Most premodern Christian exegesis took a slightly different path than the one we have just followed: the woman is the individual believing soul and the lover is Christ. As a sample of what was done on this line, we may read Gregory of Nyssa on verses 14 and 15: "The Lord himself, having become a balsam of myrrh and taken residence in my heart itself, occupies the center of my awareness." Such occupation of the person can occur because "Human being is like a mirror; it is transformed to the reflection of what it attends to" (Gregory, 94, 104). Origen had the whole Bible cross-referenced in his head, and thought immediately of the woman who "first offered the gift of her faith as an ointment of nard and for this received the grace of the Holy Spirit and the fragrance of spiritual teaching" (Origen, 160).

III

If the Temple was decorated as an Eden, fit for the love of the Lord and Israel, we may take Eden itself as the imagined home of penultimate earthly delight. The Song's poesy of sheer bodily happiness, invoked in order to speak of the Lord and his people joined passionately in the Temple, simultaneously evokes human love as it would be, were we lovers in Eden or in the garden the Temple depicted: it would be the joyous image of God's love for Israel.

Eden and the Temple are not now extant, and the redeemed garden of Earthly Delights is eschatological; so then must be the Song's depiction of love. Human eroticism as now practiced and experienced is a notably unreliable image of divine love; indeed, in the West we are well along to making it an image of satanic hate. The image will be clear only in the kingdom, but just that clarity is what earthly sexuality can and should approximate.

As to how such clarity may be approached, we may look to the practice of the Song. In the present poem, we may note two aspects that provide analogues of the love between God and his people: the self-sufficiency of love as its own reason, and the consequent lavish exchange of compliments. Just so, these are themselves sanctified.

As to the first, there are as many ways in which two persons are chosen for each other as there are couples. Western modernity has thought to impose order on this and has supposed that a history of love must be examined for conformity to a proper pattern: Do we *really* love each other? Did we each make his/her own choice? Can our lifestyles be coordinated? Are we ready? "Commitment" then awaits a passing grade. The Lord and Israel did not come together in such fashion; indeed Israel's attempt to rationalize the covenant's commitments was much of her sin in the wilderness. So let lovers trust the contingencies of their coming together, whether it was like a stallion bolting for a mare or was arranged by parents or was anywhere on a continuum between. And afterward, when love is full, let them rejoice in those accidents, with laughter at how it all came about.

However lover and beloved have been chosen for each other, let them praise one other. Let them say out loud: I like your smell—and your look and your feel and your sound. Remembering that sunburn in the earlier poem, let them even transform an ill look or scent or sound by affection for its bearer. If they have a mind for it, let them imitate the Song's lovers by composing verse for this purpose—surely the least poetic among us can find images at least as flattering as the one about the mare.

Let lovers even find occasion to say without qualm, "You look wonderful in that necklace I just gave you." Not every gift of jewels need be aborted and the money given to the poor—though of course many might well be.

2:1–7

Lovesick and Happy

I

Verses 1–3 are again an exchange of compliments, and might be taken as a continuation of the previous verses. But there is reference in verse 3 to an achieved satisfaction, which appears to be narrated in verses 4–6. We will therefore take chapter 2, verses 1–7 as the unit. It is unclear who speaks the first line: Does the woman compliment herself? Or does the man liken himself to roses and lilies? Verse 2 is clearly the voice of the man, verse 3 the voice of the woman.

The trope in verse 3 is unusually developed for the Song: it begins as a simile of the simple type with which we are familiar: the woman's lover is a fruit tree among forest trees that bear no fruit. But then she spins this out and tells how she delighted to shelter under the lover and to taste his fruit. It is hard to read this as anything but metaphor for sexual fulfillment, which then is more directly told in the following. The view that women do not or should not find pleasure in sex, found in cultures both primitive and sophisticated, is plainly not shared by our poet.

The man has brought his beloved into a place somehow designated for partying, and—preferring here AV's plastic translation, which is both more literal and better fits the context—has decorated it with a banner, either labeling her "my love" or the place a "love house." After a time, she needs to be recuperated with delicate foods, for she is "sick with love." The notion of lovesickness, whether the sickness is from deprivation or overwhelming fulfillment, is universal. Which kind is here intended depends on translation of the next verse.

The NRSV makes verse 6 into a wish, though AV's declarative, "His left hand is under my head and his right hand doth embrace me," seems a more straightforward rendering of the Hebrew. If we follow NRSV, the lovesickness is occasioned by the lover's absence; if we follow AV, by an overwhelming experience with him. NRSV apparently translates as it does in order to avoid a larger problem with the passage: the woman addresses at least verses 5–6 to the chorus. Are they then supposed to be present while the lover actually embraces her? But here we should remember the lyric character of the Song: the women of Jerusalem need not be physically present for the woman to address them in her musings; or verses 5–6 may be in the present tense of memory; or indeed the women may be supposed to have arrived in the morning to serve the couple. However these possibilities may be ranked, we will

30

follow the AV's translation. As to the nature of the embrace—whether longed for or experienced—a much-cited Mesopotamian parallel has the left hand where the Song puts it, and the embracing right hand "on my vulva." This both shows the Song's reticence in speaking of genitalia and suggests the way we should assess the scene.

Both parts of verse 7 are difficult. The evocation of gazelles and does is lovely, but how would an oath on them bind? The explanations on offer in modern commentaries do not convince. Perhaps the *Targum* to the passage is right in detecting wordplay: the Hebrew words for gazelles and does indeed sound much like those for "hosts" in "Lord of hosts" and for the "mighty ones" of that host (*Targum*). Moreover, the translators of the Septuagint seem to have detected the same wordplay; their Greek translates to "by the powers and mighty ones of the field." Perhaps, then, the oath is, at one further step of euphemism removed, an oath of the type usual in later Israel, where instead of swearing on the Lord one swore on some appurtenance of the Lord—the Temple, the Torah, or here his heavenly host.

As to what the chorus of women are adjured not to do, and who lays the command on them, there are three possibilities. AV makes the speaker be the woman, and the lover the one whom the chorus is not to awaken—"my love, till he please." With this reading, all is clear: the woman does not want their postcoital embrace to end before it must. The difficulty is that the AV's "he" switches the gender of the subordinate verb translated "please," which is feminine. NRSV translates, "Do not . . . awaken love until it is ready." Reading along these lines, at least one commentator then advances charming considerations about how love should not come too soon (Davis); but within the context of this particular poem these hardly seem to the point. And indeed, if this is the right translation, it is hard to see what the point might be. Finally, some premodern exegesis noted the possibility of making the man the speaker, who exhorts the chorus not to awaken the woman (e.g, Bernard, 51, 10). This straightens out the problems about gender in the Hebrew and makes good sense, but the unsignaled shift from one speaker to another is difficult.

II

We must first pause with one of the opening similes. Bernard of Clairvaux: "Uniquely among the trees of the forest, the Lord Jesus is a tree who bears fruit, and that according to his humanity" (Bernard, 48, 4). Then we can turn to the great matter of this allegory.

Can we think of Israel as lovesick for the Lord? The rabbis could. So the *Targum* to the parallel passage at 5:8: "The Assembly of Israel

31

said: 'I adjure you, O prophets . . . , if the Merciful One should reveal himself to you, tell him that I am sick for his love'" (*Targum*). To understand this, we must remember that Israel's prophets spoke not only for the Lord to the people but for the people to the Lord. Appropriately to the theology of a Judaism in diaspora and bereft of the Temple, this lovesickness is of the sort occasioned by the absence of the lover.

The Septuagint text, "I have been wounded by love," prevented most Christian exegetes from considering lovesickness. But Origen of Alexandria is brought close to it by a learned play on Cupid's darts: when the Bride "feels herself wounded by the darts of love," when she "has been pierced through and through by the lovable javelin of knowing him," she can only "long for him by day and by night . . . , have no inclination or desire . . . for anything else except him" (here from Norris). We may note a more realized eschatology than in the *Targum*, in accord with the presence of the Bridegroom in the church.

Contemplating the scene of embracing lovers, and taking it of the Lord and Israel, we can no longer avoid a question that allegory of the Song poses at every step: Does the Lord have a body if he embraces folk, however analogically? As heirs for good and ill of the Greek religious thinkers, we may at first take it for granted that the answer is, "Of course not." But the Old Testament is full of language about the Lord's bodily parts and bodily actions, and if we lump all of them together as "anthropomorphism" not to be taken seriously, little will be left of the Old Testament's discourse about God. For Christians, the Incarnation settles the matter: God indeed has a body, the one that Mary bore and Pilate crucified and that is risen and lives at the seat of power. Moreover, Paul teaches that we are that body (1 Cor. 10—11) or, alternatively to the same point, that we live in him and he in us; together, these teachings are not far from saying that he bodily embraces us. How these last points are to be worked out metaphysically is not the assignment for a commentary, but there are those who work on it, as readers may themselves wish to.

III

We have come to one of those inevitable repetitions announced in the introduction. In commenting on this poem it is vital to say what has been said before: how very bodily that love is which the Song proposes as analogy for love between God and his people. Much of the West's tradition, in this stemming from Hellenism rather than from Scripture, has supposed that our loves for one another would be "purified" or "ennobled" or otherwise improved by disembodiment. The Song does not agree.

We will have to say it again and again as we move through the Song: it is precisely our embracing sexually differentiated bodies whose union is sanctified by its likeness to God's own love. The heart is indeed the seat of love, but it is those hands and their placement—and the lips, and the paired organs of pleasure and procreation, and the tongues and . . .—which are the heart's actuality, at least for the Song.

There is, further, no denying it: the lovers of this poem, whether God and Israel or the lovers of the overt story, are incurable romantics. The West is currently determined to put its Romantic movement behind it; thus in sexual matters neither lovesickness, nor such arranging of special environments for seduction as that by the lover in the overt story, nor eloquent declarations of love are now in fashion. Scenes in old movies of a lover preparing the champagne, lighting, and music charm us in a perverse way: we are fascinated by seeing how it *used* to be. As for what used to be called a "proposal," "I can't live without you" is replaced by "Shall we see if we can make it work?" If someone dares make a romantic novel or film, the romanticism must be made tolerable by wrapping it in layers of irony and pastiche.

Nor is late modernity's antiromanticism a minor matter; our culture's Romantic period was its desperate final attempt to maintain the value of the particular, impractical, and historically contingent—of just such things as the events between the particular God, the Lord, and his contingently and quite impractically chosen particular people, and as the analogous events between lovers. Faith should enable us to see and beware the atheism in "cool," and gives believing lovers permission to trust their romantic impulses.

2:8–17
The Voice of the Turtledove

I

That these verses make one poem is shown by their enclosure within formal literary bookends. In verse 8 the lover bounds over the mountains, and in verse 17 he bounds over them again. This already looks like beginning and ending of one assignation, but it is not clear in verse 17 by itself whether the lover is going or coming; the sequence of mountain journeys could be fortuitous, or distinct poems could have been placed together by association. But the mountain-fauna sequence

33

in verse 8 and precisely reversed fauna-mountain sequence in verse 17 make too literary a chiasmus to be happenstance.

The whole, including the lover's paean to spring, is a soliloquy of the woman. She imagines him leaping over mountains to come to her and peering through the gate of her parents' house, imploring her to come out with him into the vernal beauties. She is to lose her shyness, like a dove venturing from her hidden nest in the broken faces of a cliff. In verse 16 she imagines their love in springtime; the metaphor of pasturing his flock among her lilies could hardly be more transparent. Finally, in verse 17 she envisions her lover's departure, again like stag or gazelle.

A single time of love is depicted, yet their union is not only for the moment. The woman abandons metaphor in verse 16 for a straightforward claim of exclusive and permanent mutual possession; in translation closer to the Hebrew diction, "My beloved—mine; and I—his."

Verse 15 is intriguing and likely to remain that way—the passage has been the occasion of many arbitrary homiletical exercises, usually moralistic. There is some key that we lack. It seems that these "foxes" are somehow threatening the woman's "vineyard"—surely again the vineyard of her body—a situation to which she wishes someone would put an end. But who are the foxes? What is the threat? Is it the lover who is asked to deal with the matter? Some have proposed that verse 15 is a separate poem, landed here by word association. But taking the verse as a distinct poem only makes it yet more obscure.

Some readers will surely join the commentator in lamenting the absence in modern translations of AV's celebrated singing turtle. There seems to be no way to rescue him.

II

Why the lover's long praise of spring's beauty? It is not itself metaphor, nor does it seem to carry any erotic double meaning; it is straightforward praise of spring's empirical, if here perhaps somewhat exaggerated, delights. Therewith the poem brings to the surface an underlying motif of the Song's general construal of reality: whenever in the Song the lovers step outdoors or imagine themselves there, they enter an Eden, a nature furnished only with beautiful, fruitful, and sweet-smelling flora and populated by fauna far from red in tooth and claw, where even rainy weather appears only as something just past that brought the flowers. Also the comparison of the lover to roe-stag or gazelle, instead of, for example, lion or stallion—far greater compliments in macho societies—evokes the freedom and harmlessness of beasts in that first garden.

34

The love between the Lord and Israel is conflicted like all loves that must play out in this age, and other poems of the Song show that. Yet where the Lord is, there is what Christians have come to call "heaven": the anticipation with God of the final kingdom and just so of Eden's fulfillment, of the beautiful and peaceable kingdom. Where the Lord comes, in the reading of Torah or the celebration of Eucharist or in any of a hundred events of his "real presence" among his people, something of the final and first-intended fulfillment opens to our experience; we are in "the gate of heaven," as Martin Luther described the church. We have one foot in perfected Eden. And there we are even now one with the Lord.

We should note also that in this poem, unlike some others in the Song, it is the Lord who initiates his and Israel's coming together. He runs to Israel and, standing outside the door like a lovestruck youth, implores her to come out. One need not approve all that piety has made of "Behold, I stand at the door and knock" (Rev. 3:20) to think of this saying of the risen Lord. The theology allegorically solicited by this passage is thus more a theology of prevenient grace than is that of the opening poem; Thomas Aquinas or John Calvin would be entirely at ease with it.

The *Targum* paraphrases the passage: "When the . . . House of Israel were dwelling in Egypt, their complaint went up to the heavens above. . . . And [the Lord] leaped over the appointed time on account of the merits of the Patriarchs, who are likened to mountains; he jumped over one hundred and ninety years of the time of slavery on account of the righteousness of the Matriarchs, who are compared to hills. . . . He looked in through the windows and peered through the lattices, and he saw the blood of the Passover sacrifice . . . and he took pity on us. . . . And when it was morning [he] said to me, 'Rise up, congregation of Israel, my darling from of old. . . . Come, depart from the slavery of the Egyptians.'" Origen's allegory is similarly to the history of salvation, but from the viewpoint of the church: "The . . . church first recognizes Christ only by his voice. For he first sends his voice by the prophets. . . . And for a time the Bride, that is, the church . . . heard only his voice, until the time when she saw him with her eyes" (Origen, 208). Again from Origen, the Incarnate Christ says: "Arise . . . , my dove, for behold, the winter is past. . . . By rising from the dead, I have quelled the tempest and restored peace" (Origen, 302).

Finally and doubtless most importantly, the woman's breathtaking claim of utter mutual possession plays directly on the covenant formula that pervades the Old Testament, "I will be their God and they shall be my people." Here the formula appears not in God's mouth but in Israel's, as her acknowledgment of the bond. The rabbis caught this:

35

Canticles Rabbah glosses the verse, "He is my God and I am his people" (*Targum*). This appropriation of the covenant formula by Israel will be repeated and varied in the Song; arguably it is the core of all the theology allegorically solicited by the Song.

Bernard of Clairvaux, with most of the Christian tradition, sees in the woman both the church and the individual believing soul. Daringly applying psychological and epistemological insight to their inconceivable union with Christ, he wrote: "What does she say when she says, 'He for me and I for him'? We do not know, because we do not feel what she feels. O holy soul, what is this 'He' for you, what are you for him? What, I beg to know, is so familiarly and gracefully given and returned between you? He is for you and you in turn are for him. But what is exchanged? Are you the same for him as he is for you, or something different? Can you speak to our understanding, and tell us what you feel . . . ? Or, in the words of the prophet, is the secret for you alone? This, I judge, is how it is: affect has spoken, not intellect, and so not for the intellect. For what then? For nothing—except that she, miraculously delighted . . . could neither remain silent nor tell what she feels. . . . Her mouth spoke *from* the abundance of her heart, but not *for* that abundance. Affect has its own language" (Bernard, 67, 3).

III

If lovemaking out of doors in a springtime Eden can be an image of the Lord and his people, what then of the shame with which we, exiled from Eden, hide our couplings? Or anyway, with which we hide them when they are not acts of sheer corruption? In our poem, one thing is clear: shame cannot be *intrinsic* to the act. In his exegesis of Genesis, Martin Luther said that had Adam and Eve not disobeyed, sexual congress would have been sheer openly enjoyed delight, with neither any need to hide itself, nor yet—we may add—the evil exhibitionism with which in late modernity shame is indeed, as they say, transgressed.

Eden is lost, and its recovery and transformation in the kingdom is present only in anticipation and for the saints who have gone before. Even the Temple, Israel's interim garden, is gone. Thus Luther's imagination of unashamed open lovemaking is carefully contrary to fact. But the acts of love, from intercourse itself to its most distant anticipations and reminders, are not shameful and should not be so regarded or enacted between lovers themselves. Which brings us to one of the places where mention of sin is appropriate in commenting on the Song: we must take no delight in making sex "dirty." Sadomasochism, bondage, and the like are not harmless deviations; they are attacks on humanity.

36

The blessing of marriage by the church brings sex within the gate of heaven, within the gate of the coming new and transformed Eden, and so restores its innocence. How those outside the covenant are to maintain both shamelessness within marriage and shame over against those outside, is not for believers to say. But those whose lovemaking is sealed in the name of the biblical God may cling to this assurance of innocence against all their reticences and temptations.

As to who initiates the assignation, this time the man gets his turn, and within a clear division of gender roles. Is a prevenience of the man within marriage an analogy to the prevenience of the Lord's prevenient grace in his union with Israel, and so validated? Paul or his imitator notoriously thought it was (Eph. 5:22–24). If we are to follow the Song and Ephesians in this, we must be careful to note what sort of prevenience is in question: a prevenience precisely of grace, of presence for the other. And should any object that they do want to be anticipated even by loving and unmotivated presence, they know not what they do.

Finally and most important, also at this step of interpretation we must above all pay attention to "My beloved is mine and I am his." Just insofar as our lovemaking anticipates restored paradise and so is innocent, and particularly insofar as it is blessed in the church, the bond is exclusive and permanent. Insofar as our sexual commitment is indeed exclusive and permanent, it is nothing less than the image of God's unbreakable covenant with his people. And insofar as it is an image of that covenant, it is freed to be indeed sheer duty and delight. Like the union of the "holy soul" with Christ in Bernard's questioning, faithful sexual union harbors a secret. It is a secret for which only the language of "affect," of the beloved's sheer impact on the soul, can speak.

3:1–5
Strange Seeking

I

As she tells it, the woman woke up, reached out for her lover, and found the bed empty. So far, so plausible. From here on, however, her tale becomes sheerly bizarre. Missing her lover, she rushes incontinently out into the nighttime city alone, an unpromising way to begin a search, and doubtless no more prudent in ancient Jerusalem than in other unlit cities. By her own account she has no idea where to look for him and must search the streets and squares at random. She encounters a police patrol and inquires, but with a description of her lover that would not have enabled the patrol to know whether they had seen him or not. In any case, she does not pause for reply and plunges blindly on. And he is suddenly there. So she brings him home—to an inner chamber again; see to this the commentary at 1:4. To finish things off, in the morning (?) she binds the women of Jerusalem with the same strange fauna-oath we encountered in an earlier poem (2:7).

Commentators have resorted to desperate expedients to rationalize these proceedings. The woman is said to be reporting a dream, with a dream's lack of consequence; or the poem is supposed to have once been a liturgy of Astarte's search for Tammuz in the underworld; or we are to be witnessing a psychotic break. The problem is, there is no textual evidence to confirm any of these constructions. We should leave the overt poem with its implausibility.

II

What does arrest attention is that if the poem were theological allegory intended by the poet, everything could fall quickly into place. For ancient example of how this can work, we may cite the *Targum*: "But when the people of the House of Israel saw that . . . [the presence of God] had been taken away from them, and they had been left in darkness as in the night, they sought . . . but did not find. Then the Children of Israel said one to another, 'Let us arise and go around the Tent of Meeting which Moses has pitched outside the camp . . . and [seek] the holy [presence] that has departed from us.' They went round the cities, the streets and the squares, but did not find it." And so on (*Targum*). We need not adopt the *Targum*'s proposal to observe how readily such theological reading fits a text whose story is otherwise implausible at best.

If we follow this lead, perhaps we may then be permitted to remember also the theological wordplay detectable in the strange oath (1:7). And—a point that for this commentator is almost decisive—the poem four times hammers home a circumlocution for the lover's identity, "him whom my soul loves," which must irresistibly recall Deuteronomy 5:6 to the minds of such scripturally literate reciters and hearers as the Song presumes: "You shall love the Lord your God with all . . . your soul" (Davis). Bernard of Clairvaux's comment here is too beautiful not to cite: "Who is it 'whom your soul loves' . . . ? Has he no name . . . ?" The woman lacks a name for her beloved because "The holy love that is the matter of the Song cannot be expressed by words" (Bernard, 79, 1).

38

We seem almost overtly instructed to take the story of the woman's adventures as allegory of the prophets' general account of Israel's affair with the Lord. Israel sleeps secure in the supposition that the Lord is with her. She is awakened to find he is not. She sets out in search, but not wisely. She encounters the prophets in their role as watchmen, but evades their help. And then suddenly, the Lord is after all with her. It is the very plot of much of the Old Testament. And at any time before A.D. 70, who would have expected the Presence to return to Israel otherwise than in the Temple?

Christianity supposes that the Presence has indeed returned embodied to his Temple. Or rather, that he has become his own Temple, as the embodied presence of Christ. Past that, however, Christian exegesis of this song, and another like it in this respect (5:2–8), poses a dogmatic-hermeneutic question that it is perhaps not the role of a commentary to answer, but that we must note.

Allegory for this poem rehearses Israel's history of salvation. Appropriately to the genre, however, it tells salvation history in a particular way: by displaying a *pattern* that is always and everywhere found in it, and not by narrating its actual temporal course, as does Scripture as a whole. Christian spiritual exegesis therefore cannot here follow its regular course, which takes the New Testament saving history as the at least partial fulfillment of the Old, and the persons and events of the Old as therefore figures of the New.

To take a *pattern* of Israel's saving history as a pattern for the church, for individual Christian lives, or even for nations, as a model by which they understand themselves and which they are to imitate, is something quite different from allegorical reading. It of course has often been done. Without judging the general legitimacy of making, for example, the exodus a pattern for the Puritans' "errand" to America or for sectarian "come-outers," perhaps at least a warning is in place. The appropriation of patterns of Israel's history for the self-understanding of other communities has sometimes led to disastrous conclusions; a notable instance is the Boer *Vortrekker* theology, the very first "liberation theology" *and* the justification for apartheid.

Some Fathers offer an entirely different response to the invitation to allegory, which it may be worthwhile to consider for itself. According to them, the night is the darkness around God, as on Sinai. The bride—the believing soul or the church—rests in the *love* already awakened for the still unseen God. But she longs for *knowledge*: "I sought him on my couch in the night watches, to know what he is in essence like, what his whence and his whither, in what he has his being. But I did not find him." Instead, when Christ appears, it is in the darkness of that same night, and in his own unpredictable way; that is, it is to faith (Gregory, 6, 181–82).

39

III

The allegory proposed for this poem finds analogues of the love between Israel and God in Israel's illusions about the Lord and in the Lord's reunion with her in their despite. Thus in this instance the possibility of such analogy is both a warning and a promise.

The warning just as it stands is a precise analysis of sexual life in late modernity: we both slumber in illusions about sexual life and rush blindly after it. The stylishly acted but unintentionally very sad television series *Sex in the City* was received by an entire American generation as their own story. Yet surely the only appropriate reaction to the doings of these young women was a mixture of the impulse to shake them into some awareness of their lives' reality, and sheer pity.

For those blundering about the city streets in search of love, we can only pray for such miracle as the lover's sudden appearance in our poem. And it does happen: actual love occurs in the most unlikely circumstances—it seems to have occurred also in the last episode of *Sex in the City*. Not only the Lord can come unpredictably to his Temple, but other love can do likewise. Better, of course, not to go wandering about in the darkness in the first place. One might even stay at home or return there, prepare, and await a knock at the door.

3:6–11
Who Is She?

I

The question-and-answer relation between verses 6 and 7 is so plain that, despite the inconcinnity next to be noted, we should not with some commentators separate verse 6 as a poem for itself. Nor is the misfit sufficient reason to emend verse 6 simply to make it fit verse 7, as NRSV does. Yet it remains that verse 6 is more easily translated in the feminine gender—"Who is she, coming from the wilderness?"—that this translation is confirmed by the parallel question at 8:5, and that to the thus-gendered question mention neither of the male Solomon nor of his equippages nor of the escorting guardsmen responds. Instead of an answering identification of the woman coming from the desert, we get a description of her strange initial appearance, of her perfumery, of her grand accommodation and its owner, and of her escort. Thus the question of verse 6 is left open, at least at first.

The mismatch between verses 6 and 7 is not the only puzzle the text poses. Who asks the question? The next-mentioned chorus of Jerusalem women? And who is to "look"? The reader? Another chorus? Are we then supposed to be in Jerusalem, from which, however, the wilderness approaches are not in fact visible? And then there are the descriptions—one using a word that appears nowhere else in the Bible—of the equippage(s) involved in the woman's coming. Commentators cannot even agree about whether one or two thronelike contraptions are mentioned or, if two, whether the second is a litter like the first or is stationary (Bergant, 38–40). To the present commentator it seems most plausible that only one is mentioned, and that this is the woman's litter.

The connection of verse 11 to verses 7–10 is again unavoidable and again a puzzle. The chorus of Jerusalem women is suddenly called to behold the litter's owner, who within the overt story is certainly not the historical Solomon but simply the always kingly lover. But where has this lover—whoever he is—been? In the litter with the woman, though in verse 6 the litter's occupant was singular? Or waiting in Jerusalem to greet her? Then we hear that this "Solomon" wears a wedding crown; even this increases uncertainty, since the use of such things is otherwise unattested in ancient Israel. We should anyway think of the woman and man as bride and groom; but is the day of this scene the day of the wedding itself or some subsequent day?

Finally, there is an anomaly less blatant yet, once noticed, even more striking than those so far adduced. The woman in the litter is said to be perfumed with "myrrh and frankincense," but frankincense is not a perfume, since it releases its scent when burned. It was, however, the usual incense of worship in the Temple, which leads to the next observation.

The first appearance of what comes from the desert is that of a pillar of smoke. With this we are surely wrenched from any purely secular reading of the poem, for in the cultural memory of the poem's audience, ancient or modern, there was once indeed a pillar of smoke that emerged from the wilderness. For of course the pillar of "cloud," as the daytime representative of a pillar of fire, was a cloud of smoke, just as in the Lord's appearance at Sinai cloud and smoke are a single manifestation. During the desert years this pillar of fire "by night" and its cloud of smoke "by day" had been a form of the Shekinah, the embodied presence of God that guided and accompanied Israel on her journey. Indeed it has been suggested that the origin of the image of a "pillar" of smoky cloud was the great incense burner in the Temple. It is thus notable that the rabbis point both ways: *Canticles Rabbah* reads the Song's pillar as the desert Shekinah while the *Targum* reads it as the

41

incense burner (*Targum*). The Fathers of the church also took the smoke as incense smoke (e.g., Norris, 147).

If we follow such leads, most of the text's puzzles resolve themselves. There would then be two consecutive poems, this and the previous, that work in the same fashion: presenting an incoherent overt story that becomes coherent when read theologically.

II

Allegory for this poem must come as close to a piece of overt history of salvation as the Song comes or could come within its genre: we are quite bluntly invited to take the bride coming from the wilderness to join her lover in Jerusalem, as Israel herself emerging from the forty years wandering in the wilderness. Narrative time then slips a bit, to be sure, and we are back within the Song's more usual style when we note that the only thing we otherwise hear of Solomon constructing of wood from Lebanon and bedecking with glorious materials is the Temple. The *Targum* is atypically blunt in its allegory, simply rendering "King Solomon made himself a palanquin, out of woods from Lebanon" with "King Solomon built for himself a holy Temple from woods . . . from Lebanon" (*Targum*). We should note also, as before, that the Temple was thought to have been built on the model of the desert tabernacle, which was straightforwardly a litter, for the ark and so for another mode of the Shekinah.

Israel's Lover brought her in triumph from the desert, and in Jerusalem wedded her in his Temple-tabernacle of Lebanese cedar: nothing less than exodus and Temple are the allegory for this poem. They are also the central theological events of the Old Testament, both as historical study usually reconstructs Israel's history and as it should be interpreted systematic-theologically.

The exodus through the desert was the Lord's creation of his people, and "I am the LORD [YHWH] your God, who brought you out of the land of Egypt" is his identity. Which putative God is Israel's—and so the only real—God? Whoever it was who rescued Israel from Egypt and led her through and out of the desert into the land. And if the exodus identifies God, then the Temple, once built, identified Israel: to be a member of this people was to gather round the place where the Lord's name and glory had located themselves. According to the Jewish theologian Michael Wyschogrod, the peculiarity of the God of Israel is that he has a street address, "No. 1, Temple Square."

42

Christianity is constituted by a new event that both confirms and adds to these identifications. Which putative God is the church's God?

Whoever it was who rescued Israel from the land of tombs and her Messiah from the tomb itself. And who are Christians? They are those who gather around the portable temple of Christ's eucharistic body. They are the bride coming from the desert, fragrant with the anointing oils of baptism and surrounded by the cloud of incense that in high liturgy envelops the eucharistic gifts, to join with the Lord.

The old Christian exegetes of course read the poetic Solomon as Christ. As to the litter in which he wedded the Bride, the twelfth-century Rupert of Dietz made it be the womb of Mary, remembering also that "Solomon" means "man of peace": "For what is the couch of . . . that 'King Solomon' who made peace between us and God, if not the one in which the divine nature joined human nature to itself? And what couch is that if not your womb, O Beloved of the Beloved?" (Norris).

III

However we do or do not straighten out our poem's puzzles, one thing is clear: the wedding of the woman and "Solomon" is an occasion of high ceremony. It is precisely the ceremony of their union that solicits the theological story and so is itself commended.

Sexual union—or all but the most commercially or brutally obtained—has been in all cultures a chief occasion of ritual and partying; even seductions and adulteries have had their ritual. Our text approves the connection. Vice versa, a chief mark of dehumanization in Western late modernity is the growing absence of such ceremony in certain sections of society. The morning of the writing of this paragraph, the *New York Times*'s "Styles" section had a lead story about the growing use of Viagra among usually potent but worried males. The story instanced a lawyer told by a woman judge that she could not work with him until she had tested him by—in the horrible but common locution—"having sex." Before their date, he popped a Viagra just to be certain of his "performance," which she then praised to associates. Here are not prostitutes and johns, but something far less human and far more evil.

Why is there—this side of the abyss—a link between sex and ritual? Because "male and female he created them," because the coming together of a man and a woman enacts creation itself. "Flesh" in the Old Testament simply means creature; thus only the Creator can make flesh. Therefore, if when a man and a woman come together there is one "flesh" that was not there before, then precisely in their physical union the Creator makes a new thing.

We are not simply God's materials for this creation. We cannot, to be sure, in any part create ourselves, for we ourselves are only creatures.

43

But what we *can* do about creation, in this case as in all others, is imitate it dramatically—indeed in the last analysis all rituals and their myths are creation rituals and myths. When God creates "one flesh" by the sexual union of a woman and a man, the woman and man themselves participate in this event by performing it ritually.

So, in Western ritual, let the groom publicly and ceremoniously kiss the bride and take her down an aisle—even in a magistrate's office if it must be so. Otherwise, let the service be a nuptial Eucharist. If processions between homes are in order—or for that matter a ritual car chase, as in the commentator's youth—let these be done with the highest style available. On anniversaries let there be a feast or feasts, and toasts with the best sparkling wines they can afford—or with mare's milk or coffee or whatever their culture stipulates. And—again in the West—let the widow or widower wear black for a time.

4:1–7

Beauty

I

Does the poem that begins at 4:1 stop at verse 7, or does it include verse 8? There is no certainty, but verses 1 and 7 look very like formal enclosures, as we find them elsewhere in the Song. An isolated verse 8 then poses hard questions, but it does that anyway.

There are few problems with the overt discourse of this poem. This time it is in the man's voice. He begins with a straightforward judgment: "How beautiful you are, my love." Thus he announces his theme, which is the woman's beauty just as such. In *wasf* style, he proceeds to praise her head and upper body. The similes are of the type to which we are by this time accustomed. Three perhaps need some comment. The seeming digression about twin lambs, none lost, probably alludes to the woman's full set of teeth, matching upper with lower, a rare beauty when toothache could be treated only by extraction. No other literary mention of a "tower of David" has been found, nor any archaeological trace; it may be a fiction within the lyric, made to be David's simply because grandeur is the intended point of comparison. As for the simile itself, in some places women still wear gold neck bangles stacked one upon another; the comparison to warriors' shields ranked about a tower fortification has again grandeur as the point of comparison. The woman's breasts, like her teeth, are twinned, perfectly matched.

44

Then the lover declares his intention to move to "the mountain of myrrh and the hill of frankincense" until night's shadows flee. There are in the geographical purview of the Song no mountains where myrrh and frankincense are to be found; they were imported luxuries. Therefore, and in view of the Song's regular evocation of myrrh and frankincense as olfactory aphrodisiacs, we are in this one instance probably justified in reading the two hills as metaphor for the woman's closer region of sexual union, taking them for the belly—a flat stomach is a strictly late-modern ideal of female beauty—and the *mons veneris*, the "hill of love"; or, if only one hillock is denoted by the two images, for the latter.

At the end the lover recurs to his theme, which—to repeat—is here not sexuality as such, but the sheer beauty of his beloved. It may be that it is this concentration on the mere beauty of her body that allows the poet to stretch the Song's usual reticence and venture metaphorical, though still not explicit, reference also to her primary sexual zone. There is no flaw in her.

II

Allegorically, the unique direct address of the lover must be the direct address of God. Thus the *Targum* attributes the lover's opening speech to the *bat qol*, the audible voice of God from heaven (*Targum*).

The Lord tells Israel she is sheerly beautiful. Does the poem suggest that *therefore* he desires her? It seems to and, if it does, poses a problem that has plagued the entire history of Christian theology and has analogues in Jewish theology. God, Christians agree, following Paul and much of the rest of Scripture, loves us precisely as sinners, as persons ugly by our own deed. In Paul's language of "justification," we are justified by God's sheer declaration, "You are justified." Translating, we can say we are beautified by God's sheer declaration, "You are beautiful." Yet since God does not lie, doctrines of merely "forensic" justification, which do appear to teach that God *says* we are what he knows we are *not*, have only been sustained by themselves unsustainable conceptual contortions. Does then God after all love us for some beauty we ourselves possess? Even if this is one he has antecedently given us? Also such reasoning cannot stand up to Paul. A very rough typology will assign one horn of this dilemma to Protestant emphases, the other to more Catholic concerns.

The dilemma cannot be resolved so long as we, however subliminally, think of God in too little a Trinitarian a fashion. If the Creator were sheerly one thing, so that the Creator and the Creator's word were two different things, then there would indeed always be a possible difference between what we are in ourselves as created by God and what we hear about ourselves in the gospel, between the beauty we "really" do or do not have as creatures and the beauty attributed to us by the word of grace, "You are beautiful, my love." But according to the doctrine of Trinity, God's Word to us is itself "true God from true God . . . of one being with the Father." God's Speech to us is both "with" the Creator and is the Creator (John 1:1–2); and if that means that there is complexity in God, so be it. We are created, and so exist and exist as what we are, by the very Speech of God that tells us we are good and beautiful and righteous. And if we do not see ourselves as what God tells us we are and therefore really are, that is our error—an error that will to be sure retain its relative justification until the end, until we can see ourselves as what we truly are.

III

The human body is beautiful—and if the baleful hermeneutic of suspicion tells us we think that only because we are human, we may simply answer, Who then are they who think otherwise because they are not human? Moreover, there is no denying the connection between beauty and sexual love. The connection is, however, something of a puzzle, since sometimes one is present without the other. In the allegory of this lyric, the body's beauty, its connection with desire, and the puzzling nature of the connection are all analogues of the Lord's Trinitarian declaration of Israel's beauty and his desire for her. What does this tell us about them?

Beauty, and especially the beauty of the human body, is a mystery not to be despised. There are movements within what is now presented as art that deny the need or indeed possibility of beauty, and that accordingly often hate also the human body, reveling in one or another way in which it can be or be made to be ugly. These are so many blasphemies—which of course they often intend to be. But indeed there is a mystery: What *is* beauty?

Immanuel Kant defined beauty as the unlaborious coincidence of the actual and the ideal, the way in which some things show forth what they ought to be by what they serendipitously already are, and insofar do not need to be improved by our moral efforts. That is in Christian terms to say, beauty is realized eschatology, the present glow of the sheer goodness that will be at the end.

It is easy to understand how this interpretation fits, say, a beautiful anemone or crystalline formation, but it may not seem to fit works of art. For are not they the product of labor? They are, but their beauty is not. The artifacts have indeed been labored upon—or should have been—but those artists whose work is in fact beautiful all testify that the beauty of what they have made is a sort of extra gift from they know

46

not where; by no accident, theorists in the Romantic movement called it "inspiration." The coincidence of a present thing with its end *cannot* be the direct object of our labor, since we have no vision of the end except what is granted precisely in that same labor. Beauty is like other anticipations of the end: they are gifts wherever they appear and yet can be simultaneously an assignment for our daily labor.

The human body's place in these dialectics is peculiar. I do not choose or create my body; it is a natural phenomenon like a tree or galaxy. And yet I may and indeed should be actively concerned that my body be beautiful. Is the human body then a natural beauty or a product of art? It partakes of both, and that is a reason of its ambiguities, including its ambiguous relation to sexual attraction.

Aesthetic contemplation of the beloved, sheer loving inventory of her or his body, is thus at once a respite from sexual attraction and the occasion of its renewal. Just so, it should be received as a gift, of the lovers to one another and of God to both. And where bodily beauty seems to others not to have been given or to have disappeared, the lover can find it— if *God* can find *us* beautiful, that is the least we can do for the one we love.

4:8
From Lebanon

I

As with the verse about "little foxes," we lack some essential key to this poem. Indeed, we can perhaps achieve little more than a few technical clarifications.

The verse is one of the more artfully constructed in the Song; it is a grammatical chiasmus (Bergant). Rearranging NRSV's translation to preserve the Hebrew word order:

> With me from Lebanon, bride,
> With me from Lebanon, come!
> Come, from the peak of Amana,
> From the peak of Senir and Hermon,
> From the dwellings of lions,
> From the mountains of leopards.

The first two lines, each of which starts with geography and adverbial constructions, make one sentence with the verb at the end. The remaining lines are also one sentence, with the verb at the beginning instead of the end, and with geography and adverbial constructions following instead of leading. All of which shows admirable artistry, but what then?

"Bride" need not state the woman's legal relation to the speaker, presumably her lover of the other poems. Here it is certainly a looser term of endearment; thus in the next verse, "bride" and "sister" are paired as endearments for the same person, which in Israel cannot be taken literally. "Amana," "Senir," and "Hermon" are mountains in the area we now as then call Lebanon.

Were it not for one stubborn textual fact, this verse should be taken as the first verse of a poem extending from 4:8 through 5:1 (as Davis and Bergant do). If verse 8 were an invitation for the woman to come *to* Lebanon, it would be a perfect beginning for the longer poem; and both the nature of its invitation and its imagery would be clear. In myth, the mountains of Lebanon were the throne of the love goddess, Ishtar—or Astarte or Artemis or "Diana of the Ephesians" or . . .— whose heraldic beasts were the lion and the leopard (Davis). If the invitation were *to* Lebanon, verse 8 would say, "Come with me to the great throne of love"; and the garden of 4:12 through 5:1 would be located there. But six unambiguous repetitions of "from" are surely too many to be removed by wishing—though the *Targum* attempts just that.

Thus whether verse 8 is nevertheless intended somehow to introduce 4:9—5:1, or is after all the last verse of the previous poem, or is as here supposed an independent unit, perhaps put in this place by word association with "Lebanon" and "bride," we are back where we began. We lack the key.

II

To be sure, if we could consider this passage in isolation from the rest of the Song, a very direct theological reading would immediately present itself. If we had found the verse in one of the books of the prophets, and if we were aware of the association of Lebanon's mountains with Ishtar, we would certainly read the verse as a summons by the Lord to his bride Israel, to leave the worship of the false goddess of lust and come penitently with him. And perhaps indeed the verse was once such a prophetic word of warning, which has come to be located here by apparent key words, "bride" and "Lebanon."

However, throughout the rest of the Song, including the immediate vicinity of verse 4:8, all associations with Lebanon are positive; in the Song, Lebanon is not the seat of an idolatry but a chief source of Solomonic splendor. The mandate to interpret the poems of the Song

48

in their canonical entity prohibits ignoring that circumstance. Therefore we are left with an opaque summons to leave Lebanon, and so with a theological crumb: a bare call from the Lord for Israel to leave where she is and come with him. To the why, how, and whither of that summons, we lack the key.

III

Despite the minimal theological story now possible for this poem, it poses a decisive issue about our penultimate loves: Am I allowed to say to another human, "Leave . . . and come with me"? In the late-modern West, we are very hesitant so to intrude on another's "autonomy." But if my *eros* can resemble God's, it here appears that I may or even must say just that. "For this cause a man will leave his father and his mother"; and someone's calling to me must be that cause.

We may wish more could be gleaned from our passage than we have in the foregoing, for the verses are in all ways intriguing. But at least under this third rubric the gleanings are, in the context of current ideology, a great gain. It is a lesson in freedom from the culture devoutly to be learned: too much respect for the other's autonomy in fact amounts to irresponsibility or even hatred. If I do not so love as to call the beloved to me, and so inevitably from someone or something else, my love is a fiction.

And fictive love is the defining phenomenon of late modernity's decadence. At all times and places, cads—an old word that has significantly gone out of use—have falsely said, "I love you," and at all times parents have therefore warned children to be skeptical about such declarations. But only in late modernity is the mere utterance of the sentence prima facie evidence of insincerity. A great boon of the gospel is permission to say, not only to God but also to the human beloved, "I love you," and mean it and not be embarrassed. Which is to say, a great boon of the gospel is permission to say to another human person, "Come with me, from . . ."

4:9—5:1
The Garden

I

Are these verses one poem, or are there two poems, 4:9–11 and 4:12—5:1? Since there is no way to be sure, we will take these verses together; if that is not what the poet intended, little harm is done. In verses 9–15 the lover speaks, in verse 16 the woman, in verse 1a–d of chapter 5, the man again, and in verse 1e the poet seems to address the lovers in her own voice.

The versions offer various translations of the opening lines, but the alternative possibilities make little difference in the general sense of the lover's initial appeal to his beloved. And in turn that sense needs little explanation, for the lines could have been written by any poet of the West's Romantic period—or for that matter, could appear on a Hallmark card. "Sister-bride" cannot in Israel refer to sibling marriage, whatever the phrase's possible distant lineage in Egyptian royal practice; here it is simply an endearment expressing the closest possible emotional tie. Verse 11a–b seems to suggest the nature of their kisses. The "scent of Lebanon" is again that of cedar, anciently prized also for its perfume.

The remainder of the poem (4:12—5:1) is an extended metaphor picked up alternately by the lovers in dialogue. To apostrophize his "sister-bride," the lover invokes a major object of desire in drought-threatened and perennially insecure Palestine, a walled orchard with its own enclosed spring. We probably should not make too much of "locked," speculating as many have that the woman is virginal or has so far rejected the lover; all that is said is that the garden is indeed a desirable property because it can be secured. Of commentators' proposed translations of the obscure word translated—even more obscurely— "channel" by NRSV and—slightly more plausibly but still conjecturally— "plants" by AV, the most plausible to this commentator is "limbs"; the woman's whole body is the orchard (Davis).

The orchard is entirely imaginary: of the products named, only pomegranates grew in Palestine; all the others were imported luxuries. Indeed, in no place on earth did they all grow together; the garden is not only imaginary but fantastic. The spring, supposedly bringing flowing water from the distant mountains of Lebanon, also is fantasy. Save for the pomegranates, none of the fruits is for eating; we encounter again the Song's obsession with scent and spice. And all this is precisely the point of comparison in the lover's encomiastic use of the metaphor: the woman is exotic, rare, sensually overwhelming, supremely to be desired.

The woman picks up the metaphor and invokes the winds to carry her fragrance to the lover, enticing him within her wall. The metaphor here becomes sufficiently transparent: he is to eat her choicest fruits. He immediately comes to do that. Notably, however, he proposes to feast on honey, milk, and wine, none of which is listed among the fruits of this orchard. Instead they are the paradigmatic blessings of the "land flowing with milk and honey"; suddenly the metaphor for the woman is not a garden in the land, but the promised land itself. This opens to our next considerations.

II

As in others of the Song's poems, we are arrested by an irregularity that seems to be a signal: the one local fruit amid the list of exotica is the pomegranate; indeed the garden is initially described simply as a pomegranate orchard. The Temple could be described the same way: the most striking feature to greet an arrival was a latticework of two hundred bronze pomegranates. And the whole Temple was an enclosure decorated as a garden (Davis).

In allegory for our poem, the garden is the promised land, flowing with the Lord's blessings. The garden is the Temple, where Israel receives the Lord. Just so, the garden is Israel herself as the Lord's "sister-bride," opening herself to him. Israel and the land and the Temple are one reality, chosen by the Lord to receive him into the world.

The *Targum* paraphrases Israel's invitation, and the delights of the garden: "On the north side was the table of the show bread. On the south was the lamp. . . . On the altar the priests . . . caused the incense of spices to ascend. And the assembly of Israel said, 'Let my God, my Beloved, come into his Temple and favorably receive the offerings of his people.'" And it paraphrases the Lord's response: "The Holy One, blessed be he, said to his people . . . , 'I have come to my Temple that you have built for me, my sister, assembly of Israel. . . . I have caused my *Shekhinah* to reside among you'" (*Targum*).

It is probably again time to reiterate a chief observation about the Song's theological story: in it the love between the Lord and Israel is *eros*, desire. If we distinguish between *agape* and *eros*, in the Song the love between the Lord and his people is *eros*—which of course does not mean that it is not, as testified by much else of Scripture, also *agape*.

In the theological story, we may perhaps press the lover's language for his beloved a little harder than would be legitimate as explanation of the overt story. When the Lord comes to Israel and she receives him, she is his *bride*: which within Scripture is to say, the two are "one flesh," that is, one thing. Whatever might have been, there is no Lord without Israel and no Israel without her Lord.

And she is his *sister*: there is an intimacy that antedates the contingent course of their history together, that is ontological. God did not choose Israel because she was desirable apart from his choice, but when *God* chooses, the choice constitutes the being of the one chosen: Israel

51

was born as the Lord's beloved, and she never was anything but that. According to Gregory of Nyssa, the believer becomes the Lord's bride by his call, and his sister by her obedience (Gregory, 9, 173).

Augustine spoke of the *totus Christus*, of "the whole Christ" that is Christ together with his church, who together will enjoy God in the consummation. And of course the church is throughout the tradition the "bride" of Christ. Nilus of Ancyra, a monk of the fifth century, wrote of the bride in our poem, that is, for him, the church: "from Paul . . . she has learned that in being united with the Lord she is one body with him. . . . For . . . the Lord, when he became a human being, made her body his" (Norris). Christ and the church are one flesh; just so the church will enter the life of the Trinity when this marriage is unveiled.

Thus this poem, even more than the rest of the Song, solicits the eastern Fathers' description of the fulfillment of God's people as "deification," as their being taken into his own living being, into the love between the Father and the Son in the Spirit. And there is a nice dogmatic point as well. Just as there never was an Israel who was not the Lord's beloved, so there never was a human Jesus who was not the incarnate Son. In the language of classic Christology, Christ's human nature is *anhypostatic* and *enhypostatic*, that is, Christ's human nature is no identity on its own but does have identity in its union with the Son: the one his disciples could point to and say, "That is Jesus," is simply not there apart from the Son's becoming incarnate.

III

In the poem of the garden, more than in the others, the lovers *woo* one another—of course the old word may well now be understood by few, which itself is significant, for the word has no more contemporary equivalent. The lovers deluge one another with words and gestures of desire before they act to fulfill desire. The lover leaves no doubt about what he wants, and the woman calls the very winds to carry her seduction to him. Yet they do not anticipate one another; neither simply assumes the other's complicity; each must be won by the other. Also this wooing is affirmed by its analogical use for God and his people.

Mere lust is action first, and words and gestures, if any, later. Love is words and gestures of love first—including, if you like to call it that, "foreplay"—and thereupon the act of love. The steps of wooing are different and differently sequenced in different cultures. But except in debased cultures—and despite "multicultural" ideology there are of course many of these—however the sequence of events is ordered, the object of my desire must be *told* that she or he is that, the garden must be apostrophized from outside, and from the garden the very winds must be invoked to carry the response.

And this telling must be done with words and gestures appropriate to the finality of the desire. My love is not one among many objects of my desire: she or he is the one exotic garden, not to be assembled to order—for these perfumes and spices cannot in earthly fact be cultivated together—and not to be picked out from a selection of gardens—for there is no garden to compare with this garden—but only to be received as a gift beyond expectation, as something closely analogous to the land given to Israel or the Temple given to Jerusalem. As the old camping song had it, "I do believe / that God above /created you / for me to love." Believing lovers should be free to say uncool things like that, without embarrassment.

5:2–8
Strange Seeking Again

I

This poem is a pair with 3:1–8; perhaps the poet has made two experiments with the same conceit, or perhaps two poets have undertaken a similar assignment. The poem is also somehow linked to the following verses; the question in verse 9 is provoked by the appeal in verse 8. Nevertheless, we will treat these passages separately, for reasons we will give in comment on verses 9–16.

Again the woman tells a nighttime story of events into which her passion is supposed to have led her, that again begins plausibly and again becomes fantastic. This time also, we will not arbitrarily rationalize the narrative.

The woman is in bed, this time asleep but lightly enough to be easily awakened. The lover appears at her door and begs admission, with epithets of love and with the plea of needing refuge from the damps of the night—though some commentators find deeper sexual significance in his state. It is not obvious whether verse 3 is the woman's reply to him or is a soliloquy while she makes up her mind what to do; in any case we discover that she has stripped and purified herself for the night. The lover tries to reach through a hole in the door to open it, and his importunity triggers her desire; thus her hands are dripping with the Song's

53

usual scents when she rushes to open the door, though it is not clear where these came from. She has delayed too long and he is gone. As in the paired poem, so far so—barely—comprehensible.

But then, just as in the other poem, plausible narrative breaks down. She rushes unprepared out to find him, though she has no idea where to look, and indeed does not find him. As the narrative stands, she would seem to have gone out naked; but later she has at least a veil (NRSV "mantle") to be taken away. Again she encounters a police patrol; this time they suppose a woman out at that hour must be up to no good, and beat and unveil her. The patrol vanishes from the scene, and she calls to the women of Jerusalem, who appear from nowhere, to help in her search. This time the lover does not appear, which is at least one bit of narrative plausibility. The final end remains open if, as we suppose, 5:9 begins a new poem.

II

As with 3:1–8, the story quickly makes sense when read theologically. Israel is asleep, and the Lord is absent. She is not entirely insensible, and awakens when the Lord summons her; this scene too cannot but recall "Behold, I stand at the door and knock." But she delays turning to the Lord until his knock turns to actual invasion; then she is wrenched within—the phrase in verse 4b appears to be a quotation from Jeremiah, where it evokes the *Lord's* anguish for Israel (Davis). But it is too late and he has departed, whereupon her lovesickness overwhelms her prudence. She encounters the prophets in their role as watchmen, who this time offer no comfort but only judgment. After the woman's confession that she is faint with love, the outcome of the story remains open. We again have before us a pattern of Israel's history as the prophets sometimes proclaimed it, different from the version evoked by the similar poem but equally authentic.

Can Israel be sick with love for the Lord? The *Targum* to this passage, adduced in commentary on 2:1–7, presumes that she can indeed be lovesick for her absent Lord. The question then is, Will the Lord return to cure her?

But can lovesickness for God also *undo* reason and lead to such behavior as the Israel of this poem? The testimony of history—Israel's, the church's, and the nations'—is that it certainly can and usually does. All religion is doubtless in some way lovesickness for the one God; but in the judgment of Scripture, human religion is just so a profoundly dubious phenomenon, which may very well be compared to questing about the darkened city like a naked prostitute. Indeed, the Fathers

54

were unsurprised that even "the bride" does not find her lover, for who by running blindly about can find God (e.g., Gregory, 12, 357)? Those open to instruction in religion's ambiguity may be directed above all to Karl Barth's *Commentary on Romans* or to the prison letters of Dietrich Bonhoeffer. Bernard of Clairvaux's allegory is precise and profound about the way in which precisely the bride, that is, the church and Christians, can go wrong in lovesickness: the revelation of Christ to *sight* is yet to come, but "before the time she, heedless of warnings, runs back and forth as though drunken with her love, seeking with her eyes the one whom the eye cannot now attain, but only faith" (Bernard, 76, 2).

Christian spiritual exegesis will simply tell this allegory and then fill in the ending. As the ending, we should adduce not only the coming of Christ—by more narrowly so-called allegorical exegesis—but the confirmation and certainty that Christ's coming lends to the promise of the final kingdom—which will be spiritual exegesis of the eschatological type classically called "anagogical." The latter mode makes a reading possible that does not suppose that the coming of Christ simply ends Judaism's role in God's history. For it posits a time between Christ's first coming and the end, in which both Judaism and the church may have each its necessity—further speculation about this would of course exceed the bounds of commentary.

Both this allegory and its pair, 3:1–8, are susceptible of another kind of Christian, and indeed secularizing, appropriation. Our allegory does not actually narrate Israel's salvation history, but lays out a recurrent *pattern* thereof. Sometimes the church, and indeed sometimes peoples or nations, like the Boers of South Africa or the oppressed communities of Latin America, have directly appropriated such patterns to their own self-understanding—the instances are chosen to show the profound ambiguity of such appropriations. For more on this, see the commentary on the earlier passage.

Gregory of Nyssa provides an allegory so beautiful we must cite it, though as response to the overt text it is entirely perverse: "Let us now observe how the Bride [the believing soul] obeys the Logos, how she opens the way for the Bridegroom . . . that the Truth might dwell in the soul. . . . [She] threw off that garment of skins, which she put round herself after sinning, and washed her feet of the dirt, in which she had wallowed after leaving Paradise" (Gregory, 11, 327).

III

If desire can lead to disaster when it seeks ignorantly for God, certainly also when we ignorantly seek for human love. Further comment

55

is surely superfluous here. And if the outcome of Israel's religious vagaries is uncertain except for the grace of Christ, the outcome of the world's sad random quests for "fulfillment," "intimacy," and the like is all too certain, except again for the grace of a true lover, who may indeed find us even as we career about.

We must welcome our love when he or she knocks, ready or not. For that very reason, we must not pursue love at random.

5:9–16
His Body

I

The chorus's question in verse 9 explicitly responds to the woman's adjuration in verse 8. Thus this poem and the previous one somehow belong together. Then 6:1–3 opens with a formally similar question from the chorus, to make a set of three poems. But the poems themselves are of such very different character from one another that, in the judgment of this commentator, they must be read as separate poems. What someone—whether the poet or an editor—intended by grouping them is not now apparent.

The women of Jerusalem quite reasonably ask the woman, surely with a slightly hostile tone (Davis), What is so special about your lover, that you carry on about him in this way? She responds with a *wasf*, an inventory of his body of the sort that otherwise in the Song he makes of hers. She begins her praises with a general statement of her lover's vitality: he is glowing and rubicund. The similes that follow are individually of a type with which we are familiar—readers who have come directly to this passage may consult the commentary on 1:5–6. The similes are more than usually straightforward—though one commentator manages to make "His body is ivory work" into innuendo for "His member is a tusk of ivory," on the grounds that ivory comes from tusks and that somewhere in the Song there must be mention of an item so necessary for the couple's lovemaking (Longman).

Taken together, however, the images seem not so much to be similes evoking a living person as to be literal description of a statue composite from different materials, a type not uncommon in the ancient world. Phidias's famous statue of Athena in the Parthenon was of this sort, as was the statue Belteshazzar saw in his dream (Dan. 2:31–35). That the poet indeed had a statue in mind is confirmed by the image's legs being set not on feet but on "sockets" or "bases." The statue is then the simile. What the woman portrays to us is a great nude male statue as an image of her lover's sheer bodily magnificence—suspect as such art was in Israel. We might think of a woman pointing up at Michelangelo's David and saying, perhaps somewhat defiantly, "My lover is like that."

How, next, are we to translate *hikkô* in verse 16, for which NRSV has "speech"? The lexicons give first "palate"—which to some commentators suggests deep kisses—then extend the usage to "mouth"—AV's translation—and then to "organ of speech" and thereupon, hesitantly, to "speech." We can see the extension happening in the *Targum*'s "the words of his palate" (*Targum*). Presumably NRSV translates as it does, with the most extended of the word's uses, because reference to a body part at this point in the poem, and moreover to an upper-body part, would wreck the physical inventory's otherwise painstaking order, whereas if we read with NRSV, the lines make elegant sense. Verse 15b sums up the praise of his "appearance"; and then verse 16a, "His speech is most sweet," introduces a wholly different kind of desirability. Together the two sorts of sweetness make him the "altogether desirable" lover and "friend."

We will go with NRSV. The lover is perfect both as a body impersonally describable and as a companion, one whose words delight his enraptured hearer. He is, we may say, sweet in body and soul.

II

The Septuagint translates *hikkô* simply with "mouth"; thus the Fathers of the church were deprived of opportunity to comment on the sweetness of Christ's Word—on which they would surely have lavished entire theological systems. They were all the more enthusiastic allegorists—in the narrower and specifically christological sense—of the similes for the man's body. For most of them the man is the incarnate Son: so Gregory of Nyssa, "All these similes for beauty do not point to the unseen and ungraspable things of deity, but rather to what is revealed in the history of salvation, when he [God the Logos] was seen on earth . . . and had put on human nature" (Gregory, 13, 384). And then of course they could make the man's composite body a detailed allegory for aspects of that humanity. So, for just one example out of many, the twelfth-century Honorius of Autun: "'His belly is ivory,' which is to say that the frailty of his humanity is bright with the gleam of chastity, and exempt from all sin" (Norris).

The Lord is sweet to Israel's eye and to her ear. She can get enough neither of seeing nor of hearing him. In most of Scripture, hearing dominates: the Word of the Lord came to Israel as Torah and prophecy and

57

historical narrative; and it is this same Word (John 1:1) who became incarnate. Indeed it was said that no one can *see* God and live, whereas Israel could not get away from *hearing* him, as nor can the church.

Yet Moses did see at least the Lord's backside and survived, if only by himself becoming temporarily divinized. And people in Galilee and Judea of course saw Jesus, which according to John meant that at least some of them saw the Glory itself (John 1:14). Jesus can finally say, "Whoever has seen me has seen the Father" (John 14:9); and those who do this do not die, indeed they on the contrary "shall never die." As Christ on the cross, the hidden Lord is a figure naked to the world; the church points up to him and says, "My lover is like that."

Moreover, the church, or most of it—the whole East and Western groups of more catholic sensibility—has therefore, despite all dangers of idolatry, not only thought to hear Christ's word in reading and preaching, but contemplated images of his life, the *icons*. It is perhaps not out of place to note that the Eastern tradition of iconography has produced images with a beauty whose outward mystery fascinates the world but whose true beauty is known only to the bride. The loaf and cup are not icons of the Lord but the Lord himself, but they too are not only to be taken and eaten and drunk, but before that to be seen also. We live by hearing every word that comes from the mouth of the Lord, *and* by every vision that anticipates the *visio Dei*.

III

The woman provides analogies of Israel's and the church's devotion to the Lord by her adoration of his body and by her hanging on his word. Both are thereby sanctified, as is—we will see in other poems—his adoration of her.

Where the mutual adoration of lovers is not grasped in analogy—however subliminal—to their adoration of God, it must over time come to appear ridiculous. Thus Western modernity's erstwhile putting of the beloved woman "on a pedestal" is mocked in postmodernity; at one point "progressive" women deliberately made themselves unattractive, to avoid being adored as beautiful objects. And indeed, when not sanctified by analogy to divine-human love, the mutual adoration of mere creatures must eventually become either idolatry or bloated rhetoric.

On the one hand, if, instead of knowing an *analogy* of creatures to God, we *identify* creatures with God, that is idolatry; and idolatry is not unknown in human affairs of the heart. On the other hand, if, instead of knowing an analogy of creatures to God, we suppose that creatures

58

are simply independent from God, our love of such metaphysically groundless beings must sooner or later itself be found groundless. Then we will either, with much of late-modern art and literature, hate creatures for their emptiness or praise them with rhetoric that becomes the more empty as it becomes the more desperate.

This page, quite serendipitously, is drafted on St. Valentine's Day. The coincidence makes good opportunity to praise this festival of a great Christian saint, in all its lack of sophistication. Go ahead: send some flowers!

6:1–3
The Garden Again

I

For the third time in a row, a poem opens with a similar question from the chorus—to this apparent structure see the comments to the previous two poems. This time they ask where the woman's lover has gone, that they too may "seek him." The question becomes harder to understand the longer one thinks about it: simultaneously it supposes that the woman is unsuccessfully looking for her lover and that she knows where he is. And then, do the Jerusalem women sincerely offer to help her find him? Or are they proposing to find this paragon themselves and compete with her for him? Both possibilities are proposed by commentators. Or indeed is the question ironical? "You don't even know where he is! You need help" (Bergant).

That the Song's poet can present the Jerusalem women as hostile is clear from at least one earlier poem (1:5–6). And the less charitable interpretations are supported by the last part of the woman's answer, which asserts, like its near-duplicate in 2:16, exclusive and permanent mutual possession, but here surely either with a defensive edge, "I do too know where he is," or with a tone of warning, "He's mine."

As to where the lover has gone, he has gone to make love to her; it is hard to say what the poet or editor intended to be the connection between the three poems, but the connection at least establishes the garden as metaphor for her body also in this poem. Why then does she need to hunt for him? Perhaps the historical-critical opinion is correct, that verses 2–3 were the entire original poem and that verse 1 is a somewhat clumsy editorial linkage. Reading verses 2–3 without verse

59

1 would eliminate the problem; but of course verses 2–3 without verse 1 are not the canonical entity presented to our reading.

In any case of these puzzles, the heart of the poem is a second occurrence of the proposition we noted in 2:16; readers should turn to the commentary on that passage. It is a formula of exclusive and permanent mutual possession: again translating more closely to the Hebrew's diction, "I, my beloved's. My beloved, mine." And we will here read it as at least partly a defensive claim. The metaphor "He will pasture his flock among the lilies" is plain enough.

II

Allegory for the poem thus read is not hard to discern. For a second time in the Song, Israel takes the Lord's founding promise to her into her own mouth: "The Lord will be my God, and I will be his people." This time, however, there are threatening others in the picture. We may think of gentiles who mock Israel in the times of her disaster: "Where now is your God?" Or perhaps they—like the all-too-gentile church for much of her history—think to *replace* Israel in the Lord's affection. Here Israel maintains her claim to be the chosen people, against both.

The church should take the claim to heart. Since the death of classic theological liberalism, with its antagonism to the Old Testament, few Christians have openly scoffed at old Israel's claim. But what is called "supersessionism," while never any ecclesial body's official doctrine, was long the church's majority opinion. Supersessionism is the view that, with the coming of Christ, the church simply replaced "Israel according to the flesh" as the Lord's partner in love, that unbaptized Jews no longer have any special role in God's history. Supersessionism is now in ecumenical disrepute; after the Shoah and for other less shaming reasons, the very word has become a pejorative. And indeed, if we are to follow Paul's tortured reflections in Romans 9—11, supersessionism must be false. There is, to be sure, no widely agreed answer to the question, How then is Christian theology *not* to be supersessionist? How, if the church is a new Israel, does she not replace the Israel that continues by lineage? A commentary on the Song is not the place to propose an answer, but preachers and teachers who follow this allegory should work on the question.

It is time for another reiteration, of this poem's and the Song's great positive allegorical claim: the Lord and Israel, Christ and the church, are bound to each other. Neither now lives without the other—whatever might have been, had the Lord not called Israel from Egypt or raised Jesus from the dead. So Gregory of Nyssa—and for a last time, since his commentary breaks off here: "[T]he purified soul is allowed to have nothing within it but God" (Gregory, 15, 439). Indeed, neither now *can* live without the other, again whatever might have been. And the bond is erotic: each *wants* the other, each *needs* the other. If the Lord wants to pasture his flock, he will do it among the lilies that are his people, and if Judaism or the church is to exist, it is the Lord alone whom they will admit to their pasture.

It is yet another truth that the contemporary Western church is too subservient to culture to speak in public, but that the Song's passionately exclusivist allegory will not let us evade: the biblical God is particular and jealous, and insists on both. When Israel and the church are themselves, they say morning and evening, "I am my beloved's and my beloved is mine." Not all claims to have the real God can be true; he has bound himself to Israel and the church. Reciprocally, Israel and the church can exist only insofar as they acknowledge and practice the Lord's exclusive claim on them. When the church invokes the Lord, and then for good measure invokes, say, a Hawaiian water god—the example is taken from the commentator's own denomination—it does not truly invoke the Lord at all and indeed is perhaps no longer the church.

The *Targum*, with its usual sovereignty, makes the chorus be the prophets, who query "the Assembly of Israel": "For what sin did the *Shekhinah* of the Lord depart from you, who are fairer in your deeds than all the nations?" They reply: "For the sins of rebellion and sedition" (*Targum*).

III

If the love between the Lord and Israel is the true pattern of love, then all true love is exclusive: "My beloved is mine and I am his." All true vows of love conclude, "Till death do us part," for I have but one life to give, and truly to love is to give it. Jonathan Edwards—the supposedly dour theologian of the Awakening—seems to have gone even further: his last words as reported were, "Give my kindest love to my dear Wife, and tell her that the uncommon union which has so long subsisted between us has been of such a nature as I trust is spiritual and therefore will continue forever."

The truly promiscuous person loves no one. The case of some adulterers is more complicated and diagnostically interesting. Womanizing husbands sometimes claim that they love their wives, and that a one-nighter or even an established liaison does not affect this. It appears also that wives sometimes commit adultery to punish their husbands, instead

61

of from extraordinary lust for the paramour. In both cases, what is happening is detachment of love from the body, to which we have several times alluded.

The gnostic temptation, to see persons as of one order and bodies as of another, is constant in human history and by no accident afflicts especially our sexual lives. For sexuality is the point where God has made our persons and our bodies one. To be a person, by the consent of most Christian theology—and indeed of much late-modern secular thought—is to be in community with those other than us; sexual differentiation is the way in which God confronts us with otherness in a way not to be avoided. The great analyst of this connection is Karl Barth, in his doctrine of creation. To be a body is to be available and vulnerable to the mind and will of another; the opening and extension of two bodies literally to mingle is the maximum of such openness possible in this life. Every pagan religion that wants to detach the soul from the body begins by attacking sexuality, sometimes by affiliating sex to fallenness and sometimes by praising promiscuity as good.

And what a liberation exclusive love is!

6:4–9

A Formidable Woman

I

Some commentators read verse 10 with verses 4–9 as one poem, taking the repetition of "terrible as an army with banners" in verses 4 and 10 as literary bookends, such as we have discerned elsewhere. But apart from the repeated phrase and its theme, verse 10 has little to do with verses 4–9. We will therefore treat verse 10 as a separate short poem or fragment, perhaps lodged here by an editor on account of the phrase association.

The lover begins yet another apostrophe to his beloved with a simile that again seems odd to modern sensibility: comparing her beauty with that of great cities. Tirzah was the first capital of the northern kingdom after the breakup of Solomon's empire, but we know little else about it. Here it appears paired with Jerusalem. This is arresting, since the Song must have been written after Tirzah had ceased to be noteworthy; or if the poem is earlier than otherwise seems likely and was written while Tirzah was still important, it is even more remarkable that Jerusalem and the capital of the breakaway tribes are *together* called beautiful.

Cities can indeed be beautiful; Jerusalem was and is, and presumably Tirzah was. The urban beauty here invoked must be the beauty more of general grandeur than of charming nooks and crannies, since the next comparison is with a disciplined army under ranked banners—we will obey our rule and follow NRSV in this translation of verse 4b, though it is disputed. In verse 5 we hear that the lover can hardly meet her direct gaze, whether because of its penetration or because of the desire it inspires. Summing verses 4–5a in a word, we can say the woman is *formidable* in the eyes of her lover.

Verses 5b–7 are then a short *wasf*, indeed a rather perfunctory version of one encountered elsewhere (4:1–7); readers should see the commentary there for comment on the similes employed. In this poem the man seems in general to be a less heated lover than he is in other poems—there is no knowing whether this is an intent of the poet or a sign of a poet's lesser effort or talent.

The final part of the passage begins with an abrupt comparison of the woman with the members of an unidentified harem. Indeed the transition is so abrupt that one is tempted to treat also verses 8–9 as a separate poem; on balance, however, it seems better to keep verses 4–9 together. In this harem—Solomon's legendary collection would of course come to mind, but that the numbers are wrong—there is none like the beloved. The grammar of the Hebrew then weaves together three encomia: the woman is unique over against the women of this harem, she is unique for her mother, who presumably has other children, and she is unique for her lover.

II

If we read this poem as addressed by the Lord to Israel, what results? Clearly we should construe nothing so extravagant as for some other poems. Perhaps three quite sober theological points can be made.

First, it is in her communal order that Israel is beautiful in the Lord's eyes. The Lord loves his people neither as individuals nor as a mass; nor is his love sentimental, despite all this commentary says elsewhere about the virtue of romanticism. As the prophets and the Deuteronomistic History insist, the Lord loves "righteousness," that is, he loves the mutual order of community in which each contributes to the good of the whole. The people who will enter the kingdom of heaven will not come one by one for each his or her blessedness; they will come as a community—as a citizen army or a beautiful city— 63 and their blessedness will be a character of their mutual relations. Neither Israel nor the church is a collection of individuals on their way to salvation: it is the communities who are on that way, and individuals as the communities encompass them.

Second, Israel is formidable in the Lord's eyes. This theme is fully developed in the commentary for the next verse, 6:10, which readers should consult.

Third, the Lord had a choice: there were many possible brides, but only one for this lover. All nations belong to the Lord, and indeed all are elect to various roles, but Israel is unique in the eyes of God. Only Israel is the Lord's "treasured possession . . . , a priestly kingdom and a holy nation" (Ex. 19:5–6).

It should be carefully noted that the Lord prizes and sets Israel apart *for* something: she is to be priestly. It was the function of priests, as Israel understood it, on the one hand to present Israel to the Lord, embodied in her sacrifices and praises, and on the other hand to ascertain the Lord's will with respect to actual moral questions. Israel is chosen to be priest for the nations, to bring the nations to the Lord, and to interpret the Lord's will to them. That is, she is the Lord's instrument in recalling and bringing his human creation to its fulfillment.

If we then read the passage also in the church's classical figural fashion, we will say that Christ's death and resurrection, and the church that brings him to the nations, are a fulfillment of the priestly function for which the Lord chose Israel. This need not, and so should not, mean that Judaism—that is, in Christian understanding, continuing unbaptized Israel—has lost her function. How Judaism and the church are indeed related as priestly communities is precisely at this writing a subject of intense and fruitful reflection, in both communities and together; a classic that lies behind much of this thinking is Franz Rosenzweig's *Star of Redemption*.

III

That the beloved is formidable we will consider at length in the commentary to 6:10. Here we will confine ourselves to our poem's final praises. The world is a harem—and here surely we may think as well of men as of women—of possible loves, but one is unique, and that at once over against the harem, in the family, and for the beloved. Just so, our love can be an image of divine love and just so it can be good.

The uniqueness of lovers for each other is not to be joint solipsism. It is rather a priestly function in the midst of and for the world. My beloved and I are not there only for each other, just as the members of the church are not a community solely for one another. The church is gathered by the body of Christ in her midst on the altar, *to be* for the

64

world that same body of Christ in the world's midst; as the second Vatican Council has it, the church is to be "something like a sacrament of unity for all humankind." My beloved and I are to be uniquely for each other, to display to the world the glorious mystery of God's faithful love, to be "something like a sacrament," of the love in God of the Father and the Son, as it opens to include us.

6:10
Who? Again

I

The section 6:10–13 looks very much like an editor's dustbin of fragments. Verse 10 may be an independent poem; or it may be the first part of a unit with verses 11–12, which would make a unit even less decipherable than are verses 11–12 without it. We have to make a choice and will treat verse 10 by itself, in order not to multiply puzzles and because something can in fact be made of verse 10 when it is treated as a very short poem or intelligible fragment.

The verse is a question to which no answer appears. This should not put us off, since the same question in 3:6 also received no answer within the overt story. Perhaps this time the poet intended the hearer or reader to perceive his or her own answer; or if the verse is a fragment, perhaps the rest of the poem provided an answer now lost. The latter possibility amounts to little exegetically, since readers after the loss are in the same situation as if the absence of answer were intended.

The questioner is unidentified; perhaps it is the chorus, perhaps the poet in her own voice. The question is about a woman, since "who" here is feminine, again as in the other poems (3:6–11; 8:5a) that begin with the same question. We learn of her only what the similes themselves tell us.

But these are shocking: the first three comparisons are with heavenly appearances, such as for profound theological reason are not otherwise invoked in the Song or indeed in Israel's Scripture. Ancient paganism saw in the "host of heaven"—the sun, moon, stars, and planets—and in their movements a living and encompassing community of goddesses and gods that—with earth's fertility goddess—was the most immediate object of pagan worship, of whatever nation or cult. It was a chief determinant of Israel's faith that she was strictly forbidden to share either this vision or its associated worship (e.g., Deut. 17:4).

65

Indeed, Israel's faith performed a radical act of demythologizing: for Israel the alleged encompassing host of circling deities were really just clocks and lamps the Lord had put there for the general convenience (Gen. 1:14). But here it is with this host that the woman's beauty is compared; thus it seems that the speaker or speakers find the woman so glorious that they would worship her, were it not prohibited. The next and concluding simile is as in the previous poem, with the glory of a ranked army—the association is probably the cause of the verse's location here.

So who is she?

II

The "Who is she?" of 3:6–11 finally demanded an atypically direct theological answer: the woman emerging from the wilderness is Israel. If, as we suppose, 6:10 is a whole poem, the association with the earlier poem and its own mysterious indeterminacy solicit an answer similar to the answer there proposed. Nor indeed is the situation exegetically very different if the verse is a fragment. The mystery of the poem urges a theological reading; and when we read in that way, we have also in this case no plausible alternative but to take this feminine apparition as Israel.

Thus the question in fact becomes: Who is Israel? In line with Israel's general relation to myth, use of the mythic similes does not make Israel a goddess; rather, it *substitutes* her for paganism's feminine divinity. What "rosy-fingered dawn," the moon, and the rays—in Hebrew, feminine gender—of the sun are in neighboring paganisms, the harem of the Sun himself, Israel is by herself within Israel's faith. Who is Israel? She is God's one and only bride.

God's bride is terrible, a heavenly host and ranked army. And since her suitor is God, it must be first of all he to whom she is terrible, whom she appalls and with whom she must be reconciled. An entire theology of atonement, of the meaning of the crucifixion and resurrection, could be built around the terror that God's people poses for her Bridegroom: "Father, if it is possible, let this cup pass from me!"

Biblical faith regularly reverses the normal patterns of human religion. We have already noted its demythologizing of the heavenly deities. And if the allegory here proposed for this little poem is at all justified, it constitutes a particularly stunning further reversal.

In a landmark of the modern study of religion, Rudolf Otto's *The Idea of the Holy*, Otto brilliantly described the specific quality of those phenomena that evoke religious response: they confront us with the *mysterium fascinosum et tremendum*, with "mystery—the fascinating and overpowering." Religion is evoked in us by an appearance that we

66

can neither tear our eyes from nor in our finitude bear to look at, and that just so is "mystery." But in the Song's allegory—and indeed in the Scriptures generally—it is not so much God who is fascinating and terrible for us, as we who are fascinating and terrible for God. God is fascinated by what is not God: he calls it into being and thereafter will not leave it alone. And he is overwhelmed in his fascination, even unto death on a cross.

As to whether the biblical God, in more normal fashion, also fascinates or overpowers *us*, in Scripture sometimes he does and sometimes he does not. Sometimes he condescends to be the object of our religiosity—and so to be fascinating and fearful and in general properly numinous—and sometimes he refuses to be numinous and is the baby "mewling and puking" in his mother's lap, to quote Martin Luther, or the man on the cross, "without form or comeliness, that we should desire him."

III

Undeniably the created male and the created female are each a small *mysterium fascinosum et tremendum* for the other, which of course is why most religions are in one way or another fertility religions. For the person of the other sex is the unavoidable and paradigmatic *other* than me, the frightening and inescapable and so mysterious disturber of my self-absorbed peace.

In recent philosophy, particularly of the French persuasion, much has been written—some of it profound and most of it rather silly— about "the other," who cannot be reduced to my concept or object of will and who just so is the condition of my authenticity, of my rescue from "curvature on myself"—switching to the more accurate language of theology, here to a favorite phrase of Martin Luther. It is rarely noted by the philosophers but must be apparent to Jewish and Christian theology: the person of opposite sex, the sheer brute construction of whose body presents him or her as both inescapable for me and irreducibly unlike me, is—short of God—the paradigmatic and decisive other. If I manage confrontation with the primal other whom the person of opposite sex is for me, I may be able to affirm otherness elsewhere also; if I do not, I will remain the solipsist I was born as. It should be noted that celibacy, when it is a calling, is not a retreat from the other of the other sex, but a particular mode of honor to it.

In our poem, it is the woman who is overpowering mystery for the man. And indeed it does seem that women are, if not more fascinating, certainly more terrible for men than men are for women. As to why that

67

is so, Freud—despite the failure of both his overall theory and his therapeutic practice—was on to something with "the Oedipus complex." Moreover, since the other sex is the test and enabling case of otherness, the greater terror of women for men is perhaps the explanation of why men seem in general to have more trouble facing up to the other than do women. Henry Higgins of *My Fair Lady* wondered why a woman could not be more like a man; that he wonders at this is the root of his manifest solipsism, which was in Shaw's original play his final disaster.

The question is: Will prospective or actual lovers cry, "*Vive la différence,*" or will they cower before it? Faith in the God who did and does not cower before our infinite difference from him, even though it lead to the extremity of death, should give us courage. And courage is needed, for also among us true love for the opposite can kill, whether the beloved or the lover; the romantic association of love and death is deeply founded, and the marriage vow is "until death parts us."

6:11–12

Amminadib?

I

Within the near-chaos of verses 10–13 we have discovered that something could be developed from verse 10 when taken for itself, in fact a great deal; and we will see various possibilities for verse 13. The same charity cannot be extended to verses 11–12.

Indeed, the procedure adopted for this commentary cannot be used at all for these two verses, since no overt sense whatever is discernible, not even one so vestigial as those with which in a few other cases we have to be content. Thus there is nothing to solicit theological allegory, and so in turn nothing for which human love may be an analogue.

Exegetical ingenuity, also that of the present commentator, has devised no plausible suggestions about verse 11: about who went into the "nut orchard"; why he, she, or it went there; why it is important that the orchard is in a "valley"; or, since verse 12 will prove useless, what then happened there. Next, the Hebrew text of verse 12 is generally agreed to be so disastrously corrupt (Murphy) that there is no basis even for plausible emendation; one suspects that the versions provide texts mostly because the preparers of biblical translations are not supposed to leave blanks. Thus where AV has "my soul made me like the chariots of Amminadib"—

whatever that might mean—NRSV has "my fancy set me in a chariot beside my prince"; the only thing they have in common is "chariot," and then they disagree about the number. Or consider the Vulgate: *nescivi anima mea conturbavit me propter quadrigas Aminadab*, translated from a Hebrew text evidently much like the Masoretic, and to be rendered in English, "I don't know—my soul has been troubling me on account of Aminadab's chariots." Given the state of verse 12, it is arguable that the impenetrability of verse 11 also results from corruption of the text.

It is of course possible that here, as at a few other places, there was once a key that unlocked the passage but that we do not now possess. This time, however, it would have to resolve not only the story but, before that, the language itself.

II

Nevertheless, theological exegesis cannot simply say that a passage of canonical Scripture makes no sense, only that it makes no sense to *us*. Moderns and late moderns, with the advantages and disabilities of our place in exegetical history, can do nothing with this text because accident has deprived it of that overt intelligibility with which we are bound to begin. This, however, does not mean that the Spirit has not used the passage to enlighten believers of other times, with their different advantages and disabilities, or that he will not do so again. The Spirit, after all, is at liberty to do such things as he will.

Therefore, in lieu of any proposal from this commentator, we will contemplate an instance of what premodern exegesis found to say, in its different situation. Christian interpreters generally took the speaker to be the man, that is allegorically, Christ. Within that parameter, Honorius of Autun, a monk of the twelfth century, interpreted the Vulgate of verse 11: "'I went down into the garden of nuts,' that is, 'I have taken up the form of a slave' (Phil. 2:7) and I came into the world 'to see the apples of the valleys,' that is, 'to reward the deeds of the humble and lowly'" (Norris). Remarkably, since there is here no likelihood of influence, the *Targum* has a similarly kenotic and moral reading: "The Sovereign of the World said, 'I cause my *Shekhinah* to reside in the Second Temple . . . to see the good deeds of my people'" (*Targum*).

III

Here we must simply pass, having nothing from which to proceed. We cannot even offer a sample of premodern exegesis, since neither the Jewish nor the Christian premoderns went on to this step.

6:13

The Dancing Shulammite

I

This verse may be a complete if very short poem, or at least an intelligible fragment, which is how we will treat it, mostly for convenience's sake. But it may just as easily be the opening of the longer poem that follows, in which case the longer poem's inventory of the woman's body must describe a dancer. Readers who decide the latter assignment is more likely may simply append this commentary to the commentary on 7:1–5.

We will adhere to NRSV's translation, though the grammatical connection of "before two armies" is not all that clear. Inserting indications of gender, our text reads: "Return [feminine singular], return, O Shulammite! Return, return, that we may look upon you. Why should you look [masculine plural] upon the Shulammite, as upon a dance before two armies?" Thus, despite the verse's brevity, it is a dialogue. A masculine chorus calls on the Shulammite to come back to them, so that they can watch her perform, perhaps a specific dance named *The Dance before Two Armies*, or perhaps a dance appropriate to such an audience; or perhaps the chorus is itself one of two armies. The speaker of the next line is also unidentified, but has to be the Shulammite herself, who refuses to dance for them.

Obviously, we have two main questions. Who or what is a Shulammite? And what sort of dance would be one "before two armies"?

Explanations of "the Shulammite" vary widely (see Bergant). The phrase could mean, "the woman from Shulam," if only archaeologists knew of such a place. If we allow for a consonantal shift, so that Shulam can be Shunam, a town we do know about, and in a special connection, the name may allude to Abishag the Shunammite, who warmed old King David's bed (1 Kings 1:1–4). Indeed it is possible to trace an extensive web of such biblical allusions around the possible references, sounds, and cognates of "Shulammite" (Davis). Nevertheless, at the overt level, the simplest explanation is that "Shulammite" is a—to be sure, somewhat irregular—feminine of "Solomon." Thus, just as elsewhere the Song calls the male lover Solomon, since every male lover is a great king, so here the female lover is a female Solomon, since every female lover is a great queen.

A male chorus implores or commands the Shulammite to "come back" for them to watch. They are not identified; the conjecture that they are none other than Amminadib and some dissolute friends of his (Gerlemann) is ingenious but depends on knowing about Amminadib, which we do not. We do not know where the Shulammite was headed when called to return, unless it was to her lover. Whatever a dance "before two armies" might be, it would clearly have been one with a real or implicit audience, such as the Shulammite would have faced had she agreed to dance for the chorus; this seems to be the reason for the Shulammite's refusal. If our verse should indeed be taken with 7:1–5, she rejects dancing in public to go to her lover and dance for him alone— surely advisable in view of what she, as described in the next poem, would be wearing in her dance.

II

If "Shulammite" is a feminine pair for "Solomon," then it has the same root *(shlm)* as the theologically freighted greeting "Shalom," "peace"; as the name "Solomon," which in Hebrew is "Shlomo" and means "man of peace"; and as "Jerusalem," where so much of the Song's action is located and which probably means "the foundation of peace." It is hard to think we are not intended to catch these associations.

But what then are we to make of them? The Fathers and Christian medievals read a text so different from the Masoretic Hebrew as to be a different poem altogether from the one presented by NRSV; thus they can provide no suggestions. It is tempting to go with the *Targum*, and construe the cry of "return" as a call to Israel to return to the prophets, represented here by the male chorus. But since in the overt story the male chorus seem to be tempters rather than prophets—a consideration of the sort that never deters the *Targum*—neither will this reading do. We are reduced to one big but vital point, as with two earlier poems.

The present commentary reads the whole action of the Song—at Jerusalem and its Temple, in the life of the lovers, as Solomon and Shulammite, and as enacted in the *wasfs* and assignations and wild searches—as analogy for the act of union between the Lord and his people. All that allegory prods us to understand this union as an establishment of *peace*; in this poem peace becomes the explicit focal association.

Throughout the world of human religion, the meeting of "the divine" and the human is anything but peace, at least in any straightforward sense. Rather, either it is the absorption of the human into the divine, and so "peace" obtained by leaving no plurality of beings who could oppose one another—as the Romans proverbially "made a desert and called it peace"—or it is struggle between divinity and its other. At the end of the religious tales, the gods either unveil the rest of us as

71

unreal, or devour us. Late-modern philosophy—which is a sort of recrudescence of the old myths—equates being itself with struggle, with violence: in its construal, to be is to exercise what Nietzsche and Augustine agree in calling the *libido dominandi*, the "will to power over others"—Nietzsche to praise it, Augustine to find in it the communal form of that self-love which is the heart of sin.

Christian faith too begins its construal of the meeting between God and creature with their identity, but not, as in the dream of Nirvana, with their identity at some level below or above the reality of persons and their difference from one another, but with their identity precisely in one particular person, Jesus the Christ. This one person's life, moreover, is love for other persons. Thus there is indeed peace between God and creatures and among the creatures; and this is not accomplished by abolishing personhood but by way of a particular person. The kingdom of heaven is a peaceful *community*.

Those preaching or teaching from this passage may wish to recur to the message of the Song's first poem: "You have made us for yourself, and our hearts are restless till they find their rest in you." "You didn't expect meeting God to be peace, but in Christ that is what it is and will be."

III

But can the union of man and woman indeed be an analogue of eternal peace in community? Much experience suggests not; "the war of the sexes" did not become a cliche without reason. The distinct roles of male and female in sexual union are the opportunity of the most perfect community possible among creatures; indeed they make the community that is the presupposition of all other human community. But they present also a quite different possibility. The physically necessary role of the male offers an unparalleled opportunity for domination—or whining supplication—and the physically necessary role of the female offers a correlate opportunity for revenge. Some earlier feminist theory's equation of all sex with rape was of course merely childish; but rape is indeed the coincidence of sex and violence, and its prevalence shows what lurks in the depths. It is not surprising that some just avoid the encounter.

How can there be peace between man and woman instead of warfare, indeed mutual peace so vital that it is the ordained analogue of the divine-human peace established in Christ? In societies outside Israel and the church, we must leave that to God's providence, working through law and custom that inhibit retreat from the encounter, and by

72

happy accident. In Israel and the church, peace can be less fragile. There it can be nurtured by lovers' life *within* that very union of God and creature of which they are to be an analogue. The church's prayer for its marriages, and a couple's shared prayer for peace, and their coming together to the Supper sanctify their union. They make it be peace even, if necessary, despite an arms race.

7:1–5
Her Queenly Body

I

It probably makes little difference whether we take these verses and 7:6–9 as two poems or one. But since verses 1–5 are the Song's most enraptured bodily inventory of the woman, while verses 6–9 make quite a different approach to her body, we will consider them separately.

The lover's encomium begins with atypically literal praise, of the woman's feet in her sandals. Given the break of style between this and the true similes that then make up the rest of the *wasf*, and given the similes' observational directness, we must suppose her to be wearing the sandals and nothing else. If 6:13 is the introduction to this poem, the sandals are for dancing, and the dancer's lack of other costume makes it, at least in Israel, a very private sort of dance.

As usual, the similes work with limited points of comparison: thus the likeness between the woman's thighs and a jewel by a master craftsman is simply the perfect shaping of both. A woman's belly, by all but late-Western ideals of feminine beauty, should indeed be like a rounded heap; that the heap here is of wheat instead of, say, barley, is probably irrelevant, despite many suggestions from commentators. Perhaps there are one or two slight extensions of the similes: the lover may indeed be thinking about drinking wine from that rounded navel. Commentators' efforts to make the "navel" be really the vulva work too hard to be convincing.

The matched breasts we have met before: the point of comparison with fawns is as before their sheer charm; twin lions or camels would not have done. Heshbon was a real city, and archaeologists have discovered it had excellent water supplies (Bergant), but as we know nothing about particular pools, we cannot tell if any extension of the simile is intended. The basic comparison of eyes with pools was and remains a staple of poetry. The point of comparison between the woman's nose

73

and a lofty castle or overlooking promontory is not—one must hope—size or shape but haughtiness; we should imagine the situation of the *Crac des Chevaliers* in that very neighborhood. Translations of verse 5c are guesswork.

II

When the Lord looks at his people, he sees only what is beautiful, proud, and utterly desirable. But surely if we view the naked reality of Israel and the church, as the overt lover here views the woman, we see nothing like what the lover saw but rather a people of God deformed, groveling to the surrounding cultures, and generally repellent. Thus the Lord seems not only to be in love but to be blinded by it.

Part of what must next be said is, of course, that the Lord's vision of his people is eschatological, that the Lord's wondrous bride is the Israel he is *bringing* to beauty, and that he brings some of that future beauty into the present by joining himself to her even now. The wondrous woman is the Lord's bride in the new Jerusalem. And this point can be supported from the overt story, for was any empirical woman quite so overpowering as this one? Does not also the human lover see the beloved, not as he or she is, but as he or she is to be? We will return to that last point.

But we may also say that the Lord is in fact blinded by love for us, and that this is our whole salvation. This blindness is not infatuation, but an inner-triune mystery. The dying Christ said to the Lord his Father, "Father, forgive them, for they know not what they do." Then the Father had a choice: accept his Son *with* those whom the Son had thus taken as his cause, or reject the sinners and his Son together. The Son prays, "Be blind to their sin, for the sake of their blindness, and the blindness of death they inflict on me."

On a wholly different line, Nicholas of Lyra wrote in the fourteenth century: "By the navel beneath which the fetus is formed, and by the womb in which it is nourished . . . is meant the church's fruitfulness in bearing Sons to Christ himself" (Norris).

III

When believing lovers look at one another's bodies, they are permitted to see the perfected beings of future glory. Nor should they spiritualize this. No doubt one loves the soul of the beloved, but the object of faith's *eros* is never the soul without its body, and nor then is our sexual *eros*. So what will our bodies be like in the end?

Jonathan Edwards wrote: "[I]n heaven the glorified bodies of the saints will be . . . most flexible, movable and agile, most easily susceptible of mutation, both from the acts of the indwelling soul and also from the influence of Christ." As the saints see each other as such bodies, the "medium" of sight must be "infinitely fine" and the "organ . . . immensely more exquisitely perceptive." Edwards's speculation is of course a mixture of metaphysics and poetry, as all such attempts must be—which by the guidance of the Song is not an inferior mode of description.

When a lover looks at the beloved, he or she may and should imagine that body—following Edwards's effusion—as a being lively and mobile as the triune life into which it is to enter, and yet recognizably the body of the same person. Or if some find other poetry more evocative of the final transformation, let them follow that.

As for being blinded by love, this has its dangers; it had no lesser risk for God than the death of the Son. But it is a necessary risk. Observers are often puzzled by who loves whom: "Whatever does she see in him?" It cannot be denied that this blinding often leads to disaster. But without it, there would in this fallen and finite world be no love at all. There is no resolution of this antinomy save by prayer.

7:6–9
The Palm Tree

I

In the Masoretic Hebrew text, verses 6–9 and verses 10–13 seem to be linked as one poem, and some commentators read them so (e.g., Murphy). But there is a problem. The following translates the Masoretic text of verse 9a–b and inserts gender markings: "and your [feminine possessive] kisses are like the best wine, that flows smoothly for my [masculine possessive] lover"—it will be seen that NRSV has stricken "for my lover." Thus in the Masoretic Hebrew the speaker of the main clause must be the man, while the speaker of the subordinate clause must be the woman. The hypothesis sometimes proposed to cover this phenomenon is that at verse 9b the woman interrupts her lover to finish his line about her kisses, and then continues through verse 13 with her own speech (Davis, Bergant). But such dramaturgy is altogether too much of a sort known from modern stage plays, and found nowhere else in the Song. Moreover, the Masoretic text of the next line, verse 9c, is by general consensus corrupt, and corruption also

75

of verse 9b, by intrusion of "my lover" from two lines later, is easily conceivable. We will therefore follow the judgment of NRSV and strike the "for my lover" of the Masoretic text. But then the seeming link between verses 6–9 and verses 10–13 disappears, and we can take them as what they otherwise certainly seem to be, separate poems.

There is no other poem in the Song quite so bluntly lustful as verses 6–9. The "delectable" woman is tall like a date palm, with breasts like the great clusters in which dates are born. The lover proposes to climb this date palm and grasp those clusters at the points of their attachment to the trunk—the word NRSV translates "branches" is specific to these stems. The lover anticipates that when he makes the climb and tastes her breasts—and here the simile has to shift, since even fresh dates are not very juicy—they will be like grape clusters bursting with juice. Her breath also will be sweet like apples, and her mouth—to the word employed here, see the commentary on 5:16—like the best wine.

II

When we read this poem of the Lord and Israel, the Song's general offense to our usual theological prejudices becomes inescapable. The Lord not only proposes to unite with Israel and the church, in a fashion for which sexual possession can be an analogue, but positively revels in the prospect; even male longing for play with a woman's body is here an analogue of God's love. This bothers us. But why should it?

In the world into which the gospel first came when apostles turned to the Gentiles, the world of late Mediterranean antiquity, the great Greek religious thinkers had provided a uniform theology for its otherwise cultically and mythologically multifarious sects. A chief dogma of that theology was the identification of divine eternity with sheer immunity to temporal events. Alike for Plato, Aristotle, and the Stoics, to be godly is to be simply aloof from what goes on in time: the worlds are moved by desire for the divine, but the divine desires only itself. Insofar as God or the gods were at all conceived as personal, this immunity translated to "impassability," inner detachment from those personal states, whether physical or mental, that are occasioned by the accidents of temporal experience. A divine person is un-affected by what happens around him or her. Thus gods do not lust after anyone or anything other than themselves—which was the reason for the philosophers' critique of Homer's stories about the gods, and for literary apologists' allegorical explanations of them.

The God who appears in Scripture is manifestly not impassible in this sense. Scripture speaks of God by telling one long and many shorter subsidiary stories; and stories consist chiefly in what pagan Mediterranean antiquity thought of as passions. To edit the Bible's talk about

God by the criterion of the Greek dogma, would be to leave us with no biblical story about God at all.

Nevertheless, Christian theology early adapted the whole complex of pre-Christian language just described. It is important to note that this was indeed an *adaptation*; Christian theology's appropriation of such language was subtler and more complicated than has often been thought. Thus also in Scripture God is indeed impassible in the sense that external events cannot alter his personal identity or character. He is *faithful*, which is the chief point the Fathers intended by calling him "impassible."

Nevertheless, it remains true that a hangover of the original pagan intention has controlled too much of what may be called our theological sensibility, and some points also of more sophisticated theology. Was the eternal Son really tempted by Satan in the forty days? That is, could he really *want* anything Satan offered? Great exegetes have dodged the question. Could Jesus in Gethsemane have yielded to fear, said, "Father, you want this confrontation, but I do not," and fled to Galilee? Even more have abdicated at this point. Did the universal Logos, when he became flesh, really "mewl and puke in his mother's lap," again to quote Martin Luther? Most of the Reformers parted with Luther here. Indeed, it took five centuries of conflict for the ancient church to affirm dogmatically even such an obvious direct implication of the gospel as that "one of the Trinity suffered for us."

No part of Scripture makes sense if our reading is controlled by the dogma that to be God is simply to be without passion, and the theological allegory solicited by the Song least of all. Indeed, in our present poem the Lord does not merely respond to his people's passion for him, but has in himself an antecedent spring of longing for her; he is in himself passionate. He not only loves, but climbs the palm tree to grasp love, longing for what he will find. How we should correct our inherited interpretation of deity to accommodate the biblical God's passion for us is a matter much controverted in contemporary theology. Preachers and teachers of the Song must at least be aware how drastically the Song contradicts our usual theological prejudices.

For premodern Christian exegesis, the lover is of course Christ, and for most of them the palm tree, the woman, is the church. Within these parameters, the Venerable Bede, for example, makes the church's tall stature be the loftiness of her good works. And her breasts, likened first to the church's teachers who feed the immature with the milk of elementary instruction, here suddenly and in accord with the overt story give instead wine for the mature, that is, such teachings as those of Trinity and Christology (Norris). Homiletically one might seriously consider the proposal of the exegetically eccentric John of Ford, early in the thirteenth century. Where, after all, does Christ consummate his

77

unity with the church? John made the palm tree be the cross, and Christ's climb the crucifixion (Norris). Here indeed is recognition of the Lord's *passion*, for his own.

III

Passion is profound attachment to someone or something, which both springs from the heart and yet is not a matter of choice. A passion is a deeply personal concern and yet is something that *happens to* one, as shown by our derivative term, "passive." It was just on account of this second aspect of passion that the ancient pagan world defined deity by immunity to passion, since, for Mediterranean antiquity, to be divine was to be utterly self-determined. And insofar as for us to be wise or virtuous was to be in some degree godlike, we too were supposed to become wise and virtuous just insofar as we become dispassionate. But the God of Scripture is himself passionate for his people; indeed his central act of love for them is rightly called *"the* Passion." And therefore our capacity for passion, far from being an evil to be repressed, must for Christian faith belong to our correlation to God.

Yet there is surely a secondary truth in ancient paganism's distrust of the passions: sheer passivity is indeed incompatible with personal freedom, whether divine or human. Passion could be unambiguously good only in a person in whom free self-determination and determination by the other were one. They are not reliably one in us, but they are in the biblical God in that he is triune; indeed the identity of autonomy and determination by an other belongs to his very deity. For the Father is nothing but the Father of the Son; his very being is constituted in his passion for the Son; and yet precisely therein he is perfectly autonomous, since the Son is the same God as is he. And the same may be said of the Son's love for and identity with the Father, and indeed of the Spirit as himself the love between them. As to how all these relations can be asserted and how their ramifications are to be traced, a brief commentary provides no space to develop the doctrine of Trinity, unless it were a commentary on Ezekiel or John's Gospel.

In that we are not God, we will not achieve perfect identity of self- and other-determination. But our likeness to God will be expressed in ever greater approximation to this goal. In this life there will always be some difference—and so indeed some strife—between my freedom and my passion for another. But I will be the more righteous and holy, the more like God, as this difference narrows. For creatures, passion will in this life always be somewhat ambiguous and so dangerous, but is a divine gift all the same.

The greatest opportunity God has given us to approach the coincidence of freedom and passion is our creation as male and female. In sexual union, lover and beloved enter each other and are, as Genesis put it, "one flesh," that is, one creature. Who then am I in this event? I am in my very autonomy someone utterly seized by and invested in another. And around that juncture, in life together, before and during and especially after—if an after is allowed—sexual passion, self- and other-determination meet and mingle in a thousand sharings.

So passion is, or can be, a blessed thing. We must finally note that there is a multitude of ways in which passion comes to pass and perdures. Sometimes it is indeed like the stallion bolting for a mare in 1:9. But then there is the story of Martin Luther, who married because he found himself responsible for settling a group of involuntary and now liberated nuns and had Katharina von Bora left over; but who, once married, became so captivated that when seeking the appropriate word of praise for the one book of Scripture on which he was most dependent, he could dub Galatians only "my Katharina."

7:10–13
Assignation in the Countryside

I

We cannot be quite sure that verse 13 belongs with verses 10–12 instead of with 8:1–2. But if we take verse 13 and its "mandrakes" with verses 10–12, reference to these aphrodisiac plants makes the center of a web of diction—to which see below—which breaks off with chapter 8. So we will read verses 10–13 as the unit.

The poem begins with another of the Song's astonishing appropriations of the covenant formula, which put the formula of mutual possession, "I will be . . . ; and they shall be . . . ," into the woman's mouth, here in a variant adapted to the verses to follow. There is again the formula of exclusive possession, "I—my beloved's," but instead of the second member, "My beloved—mine," we hear, "He desires me."

Thus it is mutual possession established in the lover's desire to which the woman's following proposal responds. The proposal could not be more plain. Simile, metaphor, and oblique reference are absent. She proposes a springtime expedition into the countryside; thus we must suppose they are in a city, and presumably Jerusalem. The verb translated "lodge" in NRSV is perhaps a bit more specific than that: we

79

might translate, "stay overnight." And her promise is straightforward: "There I will give you my love." The verses then continue the Song's regular evocation of nature as an Eden, filled only with delights.

If verse 13 concludes this poem, as we are supposing, it appears that the woman has reserved a prepared lodging in one of those villages, somewhat as the man arranged accommodation for love in 2:4–5. "Mandrakes" are perfuming it, and the doorway is festooned with fruits available for their refreshment, again somewhat as in the earlier poem.

Verse 13 is clear in its general proposition, but poses several particular problems. The first is that we cannot be sure that the plants NRSV calls "mandrakes" are indeed the species now and anciently of that name (Gerlemann). The translators of the Septuagint made the identification; we do not know on what evidence. The Hebrew word would be literally translated simply "love inducer," aphrodisiac plant. Perhaps "love inducer" was at the time of writing not only a general term but also the name of a particular species, and among the reputedly aphrodisiac species perhaps of the mandrake; but at both steps perhaps also not. Nor does the word's one other biblical appearance in Genesis 30 settle the plant's specific identity. That the plants perfuming the lovers' assignation may not be mandrakes is in a way disappointing, since the ancient superstitions around the mandrake would have pointed in interesting directions.

The root "love" *(dod)* of "love inducer" is the same as of "beloved" and "love" throughout verses 10–13. Thus the poem makes a web of diction around the woman's preparations; in recitation there will have been an almost incantatory repetition of sound. We need not suppose that the lovers actually need pharmacological assistance; the plant is mentioned not for its properties but for its fragrance—in line with the Song's general preoccupation with scents—and that the fragrant plant is an aphrodisiac simply adds to the web of love language.

A second problem: the fruits in readiness are "new as well as old." Modern commentators are mostly agreed that this is a figure of speech for a totality, like "heaven and earth": thus here it would mean "all the fruits there are" (e.g., Longman, Gerlemann). The present commentator is not convinced; "heaven and earth," "beginning and end," "good and bad," and so forth make totalities, but old fruit and new fruit make no proper totality, only a mess. "Old favorite sorts of fruit and currently popular sorts of fruit" would make a totality, but surely pushes the phrase past what it will bear in this context. Should we perhaps read "fresh fruit and preserved fruit"? There is probably a key we lack, as in several other cases.

80 And finally, why are the fruits festooning the doorway, instead of stored or on a stand or table to be eaten? It is best to admit we do not know; again a clue is missing.

II

This poem's solicitation of allegory is remarkably straightforward. In the overt story the first verse is a secularization of the covenant formula; to perceive our allegory we need merely reverse the secularization and return the clauses to their paradigmatic use, now carrying with them the twist the Song always gives. Israel takes the covenant into her own mouth, confessing that she belongs to the Lord and rejoicing that the Lord desires her.

Thus when Israel takes the initiative in the following verses, this is not what the church has decried as "works righteousness"; her pursuit of union with the Lord and her preparations for that union rest on his antecedent—the theological tradition has said "prevenient"—desire for her and so on the established fact of the covenant. Augustine or Thomas Aquinas would be content with this; Martin Luther might perhaps still worry a little about the church being the speaker rather than Christ.

The single-mindedly passionate and faithful Israel we hear in these verses is hardly the Israel whose ambiguities and outright faithlessness we encounter throughout the Old Testament's historical and prophetic books. Here we hear rather the voice of Israel as those same prophets again and again call her *to be*; we hear the voice of eschatological Israel, who does not struggle against her election but rather delights in the Lord's desire for her, and whose every thought is for the fulfilling of his desire. Indeed she anticipates that fulfillment by preparing a place for it, which we again cannot but identify as the Temple.

Israel's and the Lord's place of assignation is in the countryside, depicted here as throughout the Song as an Eden. Paradise is of course lost, and in this age the Lord's desire for Israel is always conflicted and a frustration. But paradise will be regained and indeed transcended; also in this respect, the truth of our poem is eschatological.

Finally, we must note the linguistic atmosphere, the single fragrance, as it were, that the poem's diction establishes: God and Israel are enveloped in love. We may say with the New Testament: God *is* love, and Israel or the church *is* the beloved. Perhaps indeed we may venture a step further, for the center of this fragrance is a love-granting plant: the Lord's love, and the loveliness of Israel or the church is sacramentally mediated.

III

The move back along the allegory to love between humans is also straightforward. As a first step: the antecedent fact of *covenanted* desire is the "condition of the possibility" of human longings made fragrant with love's diction and provided with love's refreshments. There has been and will be rather too much polemic against modernity in this commentary, yet once again it cannot be avoided: modern construals of passion have tried to order romance the other way around, to make the delights be the possibility of the commitment, and it does not work. "Relationships" liberated from the state's law and the church's blessing prove to be more fragile and less fun than supposedly legalistic marriage. When all goes as it should toward love's present fulfillments and final fulfillment, all begins with publicly binding promises. As for a state that does not ordain such ordering, it cannot endure, for no community can survive sexual chaos. And then a second step back: also love between a woman and a man can be and should be sacramentally mediated. It is, as the New Testament says, itself a mystery (Eph. 5:21–22), that is, a way in which the relation between God and his creatures is enacted among those creatures. Thus it is enabled and bound by location within God's people, where all such mysteries are enacted. This location itself should be sacramentally established: let it be blessed by the reading of Torah or the celebration of Eucharist or simply by prayer with open hands and gestures of the cross.

How those outside the church find the possibility of their mystery is another matter: mandating and sustaining analogues of the church's mysteries do or do not appear within their communities, depending on God's will to preserve or not to preserve them. The "city of man," as Augustine called it, is always chancy, as it depends on joint love of some partial good, which can easily become the object of individual or party competition, even the occasion of what Augustine called the *libido dominandi*, the lust to dominate the other. Where the goods of a community have suffered this fate, even love can become an object of competition and domination between the lovers. The church can only pray for communities other than herself, and the lovers within them, that they may be preserved from this outcome.

8

The Last Collection

This heading and these paragraphs break the general plan of the commentary. They are intruded because of the problematic overall state of this last chapter of the Song. There are two more or less plausible accounts of the matter.

One possibility is that we accept the appearances: chapter 8 looks very much like the repository of an editor's frustration. In a heap of manuscript or an existing collection, an ancient editor found intact poems of which already he could make nothing, one fragment of a poem included intact elsewhere in the collection, and fragments of otherwise lost poems. Perhaps he was editing what was already holy writ and wanted to lose none of it; or—in the present commentator's view less probably—perhaps a secular editor merely wished to preserve every scrap from a revered poet. In either version of this explanation, the editor has simply put the frustrating items together in a sort of appendix.

The alternative suggestion is that the bits of chapter 8 shift about so in topic and personae because they are dialogue and directions for a drama or liturgy. This is surely abstractly possible, but neither old or modern scholarship has been able convincingly to discern lineaments of the supposed drama. Nor, in the present commentator's judgment, is such discernment more likely in the future, barring archaeological or literary discovery. We will therefore take the first way and accept the appearances—though without commitment to particular historical scenarios about the editor's doings.

Working on this supposition, we will regard verses 3–4 as a fragment of the poem found intact at 2:1–7 and not comment on it here but refer the reader to that passage. Verse 13 must be from a lost and perhaps remarkable poem, but by itself yields no overt sense at all; we will treat it as we treated 6:11–12. We will do our best with the remainder. One poem, verses 6–7, in the midst of all this, is widely regarded as the Song's climax.

8:1–2

Not Her Brother

I

These verses make some overt sense, though they must be a fragment of a lost poem, on which they depended for full clarity. The fragment supposes a situation in which the woman's affair with her beloved cannot be admitted publicly, for reasons that do not appear in the surviving verses. Nor can we discover reasons for secrecy in the rest of the Song, since in the other poems the woman's love is public, observed and commented upon by, among others, an entire chorus of Jerusalem women, who, however hostile they may sometimes be, never reproach her for the attachment itself.

83

The woman in this poem cannot simply say she wishes the man were her brother, since then he could not in Israel be her lover at all. So she wishes her situation with him were *like* that of a woman with her brother, whom she could kiss in public and take home openly and entertain. The entertainment would be wine and pomegranate juice: elsewhere in the Song pomegranates dominate the garden that the woman herself is for her lover, and wine is the regular accompaniment and sign of their love.

II

If we read the poem about Israel or the church and the Lord, it supposes that in some situation her affair with the Lord cannot appear publicly. We are hindered in further interpretation by loss of the rest of the poem, which might have suggested what such a situation would be. Nor can the older exegesis help us here, since this is one of the places where the Fathers' and medievals' text so differs from ours as to be a different poem—in it the woman does kiss her lover in public and takes him triumphantly home with her.

To be sure, it is clear why old Israel and Judaism and the church have often *wanted* to hide their marriage to the Lord, and sometimes in fact done so. Had the prophets not kept recalling Israel from her kings' recurrent efforts to join the general Middle Eastern political system, of which mutual polytheism was an integral part, the kings might have led politically less harrowing lives. Had the Jews in the Diaspora been willing to be simply another *ethnos*, and not clung to a faith in which they figure as the chosen of the one and only God, there surely would have been fewer pogroms; and indeed fully secularized Jews now find themselves safe in most parts of the world. Even the dominantly gentile church now finds herself more relentlessly persecuted in some parts of the world than ever before, and where liberal societies tolerate her, she is relegated to the "private"—that is, harmless—sphere of life. Much of Western Christianity has concocted reasons to accept this relegation.

The question would seem to be: Can such reasons ever be *good* reasons? But perhaps we should not ask it. Unless we are sure we have the Word from the Lord, in the true style of Israel's prophets, we should be very slow in any actual case to say there are or are not such reasons. Undoubtedly, for example, the Orthodox and Oriental churches, under the caliphate and then the Ottoman Empire and then the Soviet empire and various Islamic tyrannies, withdrew from the mission, collaborated in false propaganda, and sometimes compromised even their doctrine. But criticism from the West should be muted until Westerners can say what they would have done instead. Martyrdom is a gift not given to all, perhaps never to whole churches.

That said, it must at least be the passionate *desire* of the Lord's bride to display her love to all the world. Under whatever imposed coverings Judaism's or the church's election may at a time and place be hidden, our prayer must be the woman's: "O that I could kiss you in public."

Looking to the time when no concealment will be needed, the *Targum* glosses 2: "I will lead you, O King Messiah. I will bring you up into my Temple, and you well teach me to fear the Lord. . . . There we will partake of the feast of Leviathan, and we will drink old wine which has been preserved in its grapes from the day that the world was created, and from pomegranates and fruits which are prepared for the righteous in the Garden of Eden" (*Targum*).

III

When we ask what this poem's allegory of divine love can tell us about its analogue between humans, the same question faces us as about the allegory itself: Can there ever be good reason for concealment? Much current ideology rejects the very question. What "consenting adults" do "in the privacy of the bedroom" is held to be nobody else's business, so that of course they may conceal it if they choose. But in the Song, the necessity of concealment is experienced as a burden and impediment; the woman and Israel are passionate to conduct their love openly. Here appears a fundamental difference of understandings.

Throughout the Song and Scripture, however private the act of sexual union may indeed be, its existence and character is vital public information. For even this erotic Song of two lovers knows that the union of man and woman is the community on which all community depends. Where sexual union is conceived of as "private" and so is legally unregulated and just so legally powerless, community can be held together only by arbitrary fiat and, if it comes to that, by force. Sexual "liberation" and political tyranny are but two sides of one coin.

.

8:3–4

A Fragment

This fragment appears in its poem at 2:1–7; see the commentary there.

8:5a

Who? Yet Again

I

For the third time in the Song, a woman abruptly enters the scene, and the chorus, or the poet in her own voice, asks who this is. The present instance resembles the first (3:6–11) in that the woman comes from the desert. It resembles the second (6:10) in being very short, for we cannot construct a longer unit, verse 5a plainly having nothing to do with verse 5b–c, in which one of the lovers addresses the other on a wholly different theme. There is surely something like a poetic tradition behind the three poems.

Since this verse appears in the jumble of chapter 8, we perhaps should treat it as a fragment. But the presence elsewhere in the Song of the equally short 6:10, with the same grammatical structure, leads the present commentator to risk taking both as complete instances of a haiku-like form: both 6:10 and this verse comprise an unmediated "Who is this?" followed by participial constructions.

The woman emerges from the wilderness supporting herself on her lover's arm. And that is all we are told. So long as we remain within the overt story, we do not learn why they were in the wilderness, why the woman needs to lean on the man, or where they are headed. We would have to judge as we do in two other cases, and say that we must lack a clue needed to make even minimal sense of the overt text, and so are in no position to go on, except for what happens if we do nevertheless ask about possible theological allegory.

II

In the case of 6:10, we took the mysterious atmosphere evoked by the form itself, and the parallel with 3:6–11, to indicate that we are supposed already to know who the woman is: she is Israel. We may make the same supposition here. Then we know also what wilderness it is: the place of the forty years' wandering. And we know what Israel was doing there and why. Thereupon the question ceases to be "Who is the woman?" to be instead "What does the Song here say about Israel and the forty years?"

When Israel emerges from the desert, why does she grasp the presence of her lover and support herself on it? An answer is again not far to seek, for in all the Scripture it is only by Israel's union with the Lord and by her dependence on him that she made it through the wilderness to emerge as in this scene, to her entry into the promised land.

Explaining the first creedal article in his *Large Catechism,* Martin Luther said that whatever you hang your heart on is your god. Here we may parody that: whatever arm you take in the desert is your god. Luther's dictum intends to raise a question: Will the branch I hang my heart on bear the weight? Throughout Israel's history, the question posed by events and enemies was: Will the Lord indeed bear Israel up? What the chorus or the poet here sees is that Israel does indeed make it from the desert on his arm.

To be sure, ancient Israel, Judaism, and the church are still in an ambiguous situation. They are at once in the promised land and still journeying in territory that looks very much like the wilderness. Following the entry into the promised land, centuries of peril and exile followed, during which prophets again and again called Israel to lean anew on the Lord and again and again promised his new rescue. Following the resurrection, there have been two millennia of waiting and temptation. Preachers and teachers can do nothing but take from this poem the theme of so much of Scripture: "You have seen what I once did when. . . . Now therefore believe."

III

Dependence is often thought to be demeaning. Many avoid marriage to avoid it. And if we suppose that we ourselves are gods, then dependence is indeed demeaning, for then we must be lesser gods than those on whom we depend. But we cannot in fact be less than other gods, since we are no gods at all. We cannot be less than our Creator, for we bear no comparison with him. We are creatures; and therefore dependence is the very mode of our being, and our glory is precisely that particular gift of dependence we call faith. For the great modern analysis of creatures' dependence and its lived meaning, readers may be directed to Friedrich Schleiermacher's *Christian Faith.* And when we know ourselves delivered from the burden of competition with the One on whom we depend for our being, the necessity of dependence on one another also appears less threatening. It can even appear as a blessing, as a penultimate experience of faith; many who have trouble with faith in God have been supported in it by faith in a spouse.

The man or woman who cannot survive in the desert without leaning on the arm of a beloved is not thereby demeaned; the dependence may instead be ennobling. There are of course kinds of "support" that demean, but the arm of a faithful lover does not. Wandering through

87

the wilderness of the world on such an arm may even be a sanctification, from and to faith.

8:5b–c
Under the Apple Tree

I

In the case of these lines there can be little doubt that here is a mere fragment. The woman announces to her lover that she has awakened him from sleep under an apple tree, and tells him that it was under this same apple tree that his mother gave him birth. We must wonder why the man's mother gave birth out of doors under an apple tree—or, in another possible translation, conceived him there—why he now was again under that same tree, and why the woman woke him; clearly we are reading part of an interesting story. But we are provided with no clue to the story itself. Can anything beyond bare repetition of the text be made of these lines?

To prevent that embarrassment, this commentary has reserved some observations that could have been made earlier. Also elsewhere in the Song the woman's love for the man is associated with motherhood and giving birth (3:4; 6:9; 8:2). In the other cases it is the woman's mother who is mentioned; here it is the man's. Lyricists of every time, place, and persuasion draw from a subliminal pool of images and associations, usually and most fruitfully without intentionally doing so; our poet's pool of such associations linked desire for the sexually other with giving birth and motherhood. Indeed the poet's imagination links the woman's waking of her lover with his first waking at birth; what in the lost poem may have triggered or exploited this link, we of course cannot now say. Perhaps there may be a further link in the poet's imagination—deliberate or subliminal—between procreation and apple trees as metaphors of fruitfulness.

II

The link of sex and birth is of course obvious—except, we are told, to one or two truly primitive cultures that never noticed the biology—and has been culturally and religiously determinative for all intact cultures. We will consider religion in this section and culture in the next.

The appearance of new human life is within creation the closest of all approximations to creation itself. Thus those who do not know of the Creator inevitably suppose that all things must have come into being by some marvelous or monstrous birth. The myths that throughout human religion appear where, as Israel and the church know, the Creator's act belongs are all in one way or another tales of the world's birthing from primal mystery. And since it is sexual union from which birth observably proceeds, this mystery, "fascinating and terrible"—see the commentary to 6:10—will be told as the story of a primal coupling, often of the Sun God and Mother Earth. Indeed, all non-Abrahamic religion is finally fertility religion.

Theological use of the Song thus has a boundary it must always respect and fear. However drastically and imaginatively we may allegorically evoke the erotic love and union between the Lord and his people, we must keep well away from envisaging Israel or the church as bearing forth the creation. Nor can we suppose ourselves in no danger of doing so. Theology has in the past drawn dangerously from philosophies that are in fact sublimations of the old myths, that construe the world as *emanating* from a mysterious first principle. As for the "new age" thought with which some contemporary theology has flirted, it is not even a sublimation of old fertility religion, but rather a degenerate and crude version of it.

III

The bond of sexual union between male and female in one generation and the bond of descent across generations, perhaps indeed of descent through generations of ancestors, are known and practiced as one bond in the *family*. The structure of the family varies widely from one culture to another, but all cultures have understood that the link it constitutes between union in one generation and union across generations is the foundation of all political and societal community. Thus rituals of marriage and birth again vary widely from culture to culture, but all somehow enforce this link between the two, all somehow enforce the family—even by "transgressing" it.

The previous paragraph holds, to be sure, only for cultures earlier than the late-Western culture of birth prevention. We cannot predict what must come of a culture that altogether severs the link between sexual union and birth—or rather we must hope we cannot predict it, since Aldous Huxley's *Brave New World* looks very much like being the prediction to be made. A childless marriage is still a marriage, and the childlessness can even be a blessing, as a suffering born. But a deliberately childless union is an offense against society; and a society that cultivates such unions is a stumbling block to itself.

8:6–7
The Power of Love

I

The opening lines of this poem are in the voice of the woman, and there is no reason to suppose a change of voice later. Nor is there any reason to suppose these verses are not a complete poem—though of course we cannot be sure they are.

The woman speaks to her lover, with a radical and wonderful demand. Then she justifies making it. The content and mode of the lines in which she does the latter are unique in the Song, for here and only here the Song lauds love itself, directly and as such.

The woman's request is to be her lover's seal. In the ancient world and later, a person's seal was the statement and guarantee of his identity. When handwriting was not individual as it has since become, and indeed great rulers could not write, a signature did not prove who had signed a document; but a person's seal could be unique. It was kept close by the person, in a purse or under outer garments, in our poem on a cord around the neck or bound to an arm. In medieval Europe, if a messenger had to be sent with an urgent message whose origin might not be believed, the messenger might, if greatly trusted, be given the sender's seal to carry and show.

We do not have here a simile; the woman wants to *be* her lover's seal (Bergant). That is, she asks him to take her as the visible mark and surety of his own identity; she petitions to be indispensable to his being who he is. In other Old Testament language, they are to be "one flesh," one identifiable person over against all others. But what makes such a request reasonable? How can one person be intrinsic to the identity of another?

In verses 6c–7 the woman proclaims why and how that can be. It is not at first sight obvious that these lines, grand as they are in poetic form and rhetoric, actually support her claim. We must work step by step.

First, we must provide our own translation of verse 6b, for the poetic form is vital, and to see it we need to retain the Hebrew word order. Nor should we with NRSV generalize the second line by translating *qinah* "passion" instead of AV's "jealousy"; *qinah* is specifically the implacability and exclusivity of a passionate attachment, and we are surely meant to overhear, "I the LORD your God am a jealous God," who brook no rivals (Ex. 20:5). We will read: "For strong as death is love; fierce as the grave is jealousy." The two lines make a classic unit of Hebrew poetry: two lines parallel in both grammar and statement, each line with three accented words, in pairs. "Strong" and "fierce" reinforce each other, as do "death" and "the grave." The exegetical question has then been: Are "love" and "jealousy" paired to reinforce each other or to contrast with each other? Is jealousy here a good thing or a bad thing?

Hebrew poetry knows both modes of parallelism; and much commentary proposes the second reading. But, in the present commentator's view, two considerations establish that the lines are in reinforcing rather than antithetical parallelism. First, if jealousy is here the passion of a lover's exclusive title in the beloved, then the proposition that this passion is "fierce" directly supports the woman's opening claim, which is what she puts it forward to do. Second, the next sentence begins, "Its flashes . . ." What is the antecedent of the singular possessive? Much the easiest construal makes the antecedent be "love" and "jealousy" taken as one thing.

The word order of the couplet's first line presents us first with death's strength. Death is absolute; one cannot negotiate with it—despite all the stories about attempts to do so. It takes whom it takes when it takes them, and none can finally resist. Love, the woman then says, is like that: her claim on her lover is not negotiable even by him; she will be the very seal of his identity.

The word order of the second line is the same. The grave is fierce, absolute in its own way. It does not give up those whom it has taken—except perhaps as unwilling voices of doom, like Samuel called by the witch of Endor (1 Sam. 28:7–18). Jealousy is then that aspect of love in which love also does not give up what it claims; and, says the woman, loving jealousy is as tenacious in this as the grave itself. No one can slough off his or her identity; no more will her lover slough off her.

But now we must note that these considerations only explain what moves the woman's claim; they do not justify it. They do not establish that the woman's love enables her to be in fact the seal of her lover's identity. For death will—it surely appears—part them; even the classic wedding promise is "till death do us part." It is not established that the woman's jealousy will be as fierce as the grave's; for the grave's hold will—it surely appears—eventually triumph over hers. We have arrived at a contest implied in the comparisons: love is strong *as* death; jealousy as fierce *as* the grave. Our verses set up a contest between love and death, jealousy and the grave.

The woman's claim is justified only if love defeats death, if lovers' jealousy defeats the grave. It is sometimes argued by commentators that our poem does not say that love is stronger than death, only that it is *as* strong as death. But this is a distinction without a difference. For death does not allow of stalemates. If love binds lovers even in death's despite, then love is in fact the stronger. If love is not overcome by death, then death is overcome by love. Nor does the grave allow of partial retrievals; if it yields its prey, then its jealousy is defeated and not merely matched.

The remaining lines continue the theme of love's invincibility. Its lightning strikes—a regular image of love poetry—are true fire, superlative fire, which no flood can quench. Not even wealth can corrupt it.

If love's strength is indeed greater than death's and loving jealousy's grip more tenacious than the grave's, then the woman is not only in fact moved to make her claim, but has reason for its validity. But are these things true? We want them to be, but are they? Does not death in fact sever lovers, many before their love is ripened and all eventually? And once the beloved is dead, is not the lover alone at the grave? Does not disaster, such as "many waters," often undo love? And does not money undo it more often? Whose love, exactly, defeats death and natural evil and mammon? In the overt story, the woman claims it is her love, and we honor her audacity—an audacity which, we may finally note, undergirds the whole Song.

II

A second look at the language of this poem suggests, however, another answer to the question just posed. For translation conceals the poem's pervading reference to the myths of Israel's religious milieu. *Mot* can indeed be translated simply "death," but it is also a proper name, for the Canaanite god with whom Baal, the giver of life, must struggle. *Sheol* can be translated "grave," but it is also the Old Testament's standard word for the underworld of shadows, which in the myths around Israel and in Israel's own poesy is often personified as grasping for humans. *Resep* is "flame," but is also the name of the Canaanite god of pestilence (Bergant); according to our poem, love's flame is the flame of flames, a superlative flame, which *resep* is not. As for the "many waters" that cannot quench love, they are the Old Testament's standard and frequent representation of that Chaos which battles against the Creator (Murphy). Finally, although here the word for wealth is not "Mammon," surely we are justified in lining wealth up with the rest. It is with these very powers, headed by Death and Sheol, that Jerusalem's apostate rulers, according to Isaiah 28, made covenant against the Lord.

Surely it is only *God's* love that can be equal to these mythic powers. *Canticles Rabbah* makes the identification: "'Cannot quench love.' This is the love which the Holy One, blessed be he, has for Israel" (*Targum*). And God's love is victorious; "O death, where is thy sting? O grave, where is thy victory?" (1 Cor. 15:55). If in allegory for this poem the woman is Israel, as in the rest of the Song, then Israel does not here appeal to her own love but to that of her Lover.

The proclamation that "jealousy" defeats the grave is a very direct and central theological proposition of the Old Testament: it belongs to the foundation of Israel's life, the "Ten Words" of the covenant given at Sinai, that the Lord is "a jealous God" (Ex. 20:5; Deut. 4:24). Indeed, the Lord can have "Jealous" as a personal name (Ex. 34:14)! For like a jealous spouse, the Lord will not share his people with any other power. Modernity balks at that, but in fact all our salvation lies in it, for other powers do not save—or perhaps they each indeed produce what they promise, but these are "salvations" very different than the Life and Kingdom and Health and Order and Plenty given by the Lord's victory over Death and Grave and Pestilence and Chaos and Mammon. Indeed, the gods of the nations *are* Death, Grave, Pestilence, Chaos, and Mammon.

Christian preaching or teaching of this poem must center around Christ's Resurrection, his victory over death and death's allies, and around its guarantee of our own rescue from them. His death has made us the seal of his identity: he died "for" us, in identification with us. Now he is not who he is without us; he did not go into death without us, and he will not fulfill his Resurrection without us. Indeed, whatever might have been, our reality as the seal of his identity is such that as the risen one he *cannot* be himself without us. Bernard of Clairvaux, in comment on a different passage of the Song, made the vital Pauline point about why the Lord's love is so strong and fierce: "He loved us before we existed; and went beyond that to love us when we resisted him. . . . Indeed, had he not loved his enemies he would have no friends" (Bernard, 20, 2). Just so, the Lord will not share us with other lords, of whom notoriously there are many. Christ, we may say, is Jealousy incarnate.

Augustine wrote, "Just as death achieves heights of fury in the work of destruction, so love achieves heights of fury in the work of salvation." And Honorius of Autun in the twelfth century gave Augustine's antitheses a powerful soteriological twist, putting them in the mouth of Christ: "Just as death overpowers all the mighty, and therefore is mightier than all, so too love is mightier than all—that has overpowered me who am the mightiest, and brought me to death for your sake" (Norris).

93

III

The connection of love and death is deeply embedded in our culture—"You always hurt the one you love," and the hurt tends to death, "till the petals fall." Vice versa, lovers have immemorially maintained their willingness themselves to die rather than be dispossessed of the beloved. Putting the two together: "I kissed thee ere I killed thee. No way but this: Killing myself, to die upon a kiss." The connection between love and death is located in that dual nature of love as both gift, *agape*, and desire, *eros*, which underlies our whole exposition of the Song.

Insofar as love is gift, to love is not to give something or several somethings; it is to give myself. If I give gifts in the plural, these are but tokens of the one thing I really have to give, myself. If I forget, and send no roses for St. Valentine's festival, this does not wound unless it is a negative token, of forgetfulness of the beloved.

But how can I give myself as *gift?* Whether inflicting myself on another is gift or curse depends on who and what I am; even his followers ran from Stalin's affections. But who and what I am is not determined until "the moving finger" has written the last line of my story, and then I am not around to make the gift. Postmodern philosophers have noted this, and simply equated love as gift with—finally futile—total sacrifice.

Insofar as love is desire, to love is not to desire one thing or another of the beloved; it is simply to desire the beloved's own person. The beloved, however, will have the same difficulty in making such a gift as was just described in the first person. Moreover, there is death in the desire to have the object of love whole. It is by no linguistic accident that we speak of love that "eats up" the beloved—as one who loves lobster may devour the whole beast, and then has no lobster left.

How can I desire the beloved whole, without destroying his or her being? How can I desire simply the beloved without reducing him or her to an appendage or reproduction of myself? It is not without reason that those who find themselves loved sometimes flee even when they know they might come in turn to love, indeed that some spend their lives in such flight.

If there were not the supreme act of the Lord's love for his people, the crucifixion and Resurrection of Israel's Christ, the prudent advice might indeed be to keep clear of love. But cross and Resurrection are the fact, and that puts love and death into a new relation. Does the gift of love lead to the death of the lover? Yes, it led Christ to death for us. Does the desire of love lead to the death of the beloved? Yes, Christ's desire for us took and takes us with him into death: "we have been buried with him by baptism into death" (Rom. 6:4).

And together Christ's gift and desire led to life in love, because there is also the Father. The desire of the Father for the Son raised him from the death in which his self-giving to his people completed itself; thus in spite of having lived out his life for us to the end, he nevertheless lives to give the gift. Vice versa, we are not the Son's by his sheer desire for us, but are rather the Father's gift to the Son (e.g., John 17:6), and that means that the Son's desire for us can be total without being devouring.

We could go on with these dialectics for many pages; and none of this quite works without the Spirit, whom we have not invoked. But perhaps this is enough to show why those who are bound into the multifarious love between the Father and Son are safe from the postmodernists' grim diagnosis. We can take the risk of giving ourselves to the beloved and of loving the beloved's own self. There is death in that, but it is death unto new life.

The question then arises again: How does love occur outside Israel's and the church's union with the Lord? For manifestly it does. And as elsewhere in this commentary (6:9–13), we can only say: wherever by God's providence love happens, the love between the Father and the Son and the Son's love of sinners are its "condition of possibility." The synagogue and church have the great advantage that they know this and can live by it.

In that knowledge, each of us can with clear conscience say to the beloved, "Make me your seal, the mark of your identity." Exactly how such union will, in Jonathan Edwards's words, "continue forever" (6:1–3) we do not know, but the Song says that somehow it will.

8:8–10
The Little Sister Grows Up

I

Do verses 8–9 and 10 make one unit or two? Much supports their division. What connects verse 10 with verses 8–9 is mostly mention of breasts, walls, and battlements; and the collocation of the verses may thus be occasioned only by word association, for whereas the battlements to be built in verse 9 are metaphor for honor and power, the towers of verse

10 are simile for the woman's breasts themselves. Verses 8–9 are the voice of a male chorus, and verse 10 is the voice of the Song's passionate woman; for the two speeches to be an exchange they must somehow come together over the time it takes for the prepubescent girl spoken of in verses 8–9 to become the mature woman who speaks in verse 10.

Nevertheless, one cannot easily overcome the impression that these verses are not placed together by word association only. Perhaps this time we do have something like a dramatic scene, or part of one. And one very definite consideration does argue for verses 8–10 as the unit: verses 8–9 by themselves would be the only poem in the Song in which neither the woman of 1:1 nor her lover plausibly appears, whether as speaker, addressee, or topic. That could be explained by taking verses 8–9 as a fragment, but where we do not have to make that judgment we should not. Not quite just flipping a coin, we will take verses 8–10 as a dramatic whole.

An unidentified chorus of brothers has a little sister. She has as yet no breasts. In the present commentator's view, we should take this to mean simply that she is too young for marriage, which in the ancient Near East was the same as being too young for sexual activity. One day, however, she will be old enough for proposals of marriage, that is, for sex. It is the advent of the latter about which the brothers are concerned. What will they do then? Here the tropes begin.

The sister will on that day prove to be either a wall or a door; what these metaphors suggest is surely plain enough. If on that day she shows herself secure against temptation, they will crown her virtue with silver battlements. If she is vulnerable, they will wall her in. The materials named, particularly cedar, are prominent among the precious materials that appear throughout the Song; even if the brothers decide to restrain their sister, they will do it grandly.

Verse 10 makes a fast forward: the sister speaks in her own voice and as decidedly grown-up. Responding to her brothers' previous worries by mixing their metaphors, she first attests her virtue; when the time of testing came she was a wall and no open door. Then she proclaims a triumphant sexuality, for she indeed has breasts, like towers of the battlements the brothers contemplated.

Now she appears as the passionate and beloved woman of the other poems: it is in her lover's eyes that her splendid breasts are valued. They make her for him a "bringer of peace"; if we have the poem complete, "peace" is then its final word. Thus the little drama is tied into the web of names and allusions around the root *shlm* which appears in the latter chapters of the Song; in the woman of this poem we meet again the Shulammite, the female sovereign of peace (6:13).

96

II

When we read this poem as a solicitation of theological allegory, we must cast Israel or the church as the sister. Then the allegory cannot avoid what with the Song is usually not appropriate, some narration of salvation history. We will most attend to two theological propositions posed by this version of salvation history. Both are arresting; preachers and teachers should think long before adopting—or rejecting—either of them.

In allegory, the speech of the brothers sets us in a time when Israel was not yet united to the Lord, the time before the exodus and the covenant at Sinai. The chorus looks forward to choices that will be posed to Israel when her time comes: when she will have to unite chastely with her Lord or go after other gods, when she will either follow Moses out of Egypt or stay put, when she must say yes or no to the covenant. And here we encounter the first theological challenge: looking forward, the theological story supposes that Israel might make the wrong choice.

What if Israel had not merely had moments of reluctance, but had simply refused to follow Moses? What if when, as *Canticles Rabbah* has it, the commandment came to each Israelite asking for the promise of obedience (1:1) they had said no? What if Mary had said, "I want no part of this strange seduction"? What if Jesus had fallen to the tempter? What indeed if the church should now succeed in carrying out her apparent determination to apostasize? When the Lord comes, will he find faith on the earth? If these are real questions, must we then say, with several contemporary theologians—we must mention at least Wolfhart Pannenberg—that when the history of God's people confronts her with such decisions, the Lord's own deity hangs in the balance? If we accept that daunting proposition, concepts intrinsic to our inherited construal of God—particularly omnipotence and omniscience—will need revisiting.

Still to scene one of the drama: Who are the brothers? In the overt story, they are probably to be identified with the brothers of chapter 2, who disciplined the woman by putting her to field labor. Who should they be in the allegory? The *Targum* makes them be the angels, which indeed is an appropriate suggestion: in Scripture various heavenly beings appear as elders within God's creation and as guardians of other creatures (*Targum*). And for the angels to be observing the progress of salvation history and meditating what is to be done is well within the Bible's view of things.

The second scene is set in the time when the union of the Lord and his people has been concluded, the time of Israel or the time of the

97

church. The crux envisioned by the brothers has come and is past. God's people have made their choice, and all is insofar well.

A second arresting supposition of this theological drama is suggested by an allusion in the overt text so blatant it is hard to think the poet did not intend us to catch it. The woman claims to be—in more literal translation—a "peace-bringing one" for the lover. But throughout the prophetic literature peace bringing is a chief attribute of the Messiah; and "peace-bringing one" is too like the great title itself, "Prince of Peace" (Isa. 9:6), for the parallel to be ignored. Shockingly, in the allegory the relations as they appear elsewhere in Scripture are reversed: Israel claims the role of peace bringer, and the Lord is the one to whom she brings peace. The question is: Can such reciprocity be affirmed? The Lord and his Messiah can bring peace to the people, but can Israel or the church bring peace to the Lord?

As is regularly noted, *shalom* is not just the opposite of strife but wholeness in the sense of completion. I am at peace when I make one whole with God and my neighbor and just so with myself, when I am *at one* with all of these. If now the Lord truly desires his people, if his love for them is *eros*—as the allegory solicited by the Song insists at every step—then when his people are at one with him, when his desire is satisfied, this is not only their peace but indeed must somehow be his.

It is an ancient theological problem, to which all answers are equally upsetting: Can God make a whole with creatures, a whole that somehow *satisfies* him? If he cannot, why are there creatures? If he can, does this not imply that in himself he lacks something? Why indeed should God have a creation at all? What does he need it for? Most theologians have seen the problem, and many have avoided facing it. Jonathan Edwards was several times invoked earlier in this commentary; and here we may again commend his thinking in the *Dissertation Concerning the End for Which God Created the World*. Drastically summarizing Edwards's subtle dialectics: given the fact of God's eternal election, behind which we cannot penetrate, our good and God's good are from his side indistinguishable.

III

The turn back to the human analogy is then as immediately suggested as is the theological story itself. First, when the possibility of loving union is proposed, there is a decision to be made, and it is possible to make the wrong one. Moreover, however we may want to describe the decision to ourselves, it is never really a decision between alternative loves, but is rather between love and something less. We are offered love, and we either find courage for it or we do not. We are confronted with that formidable other—see the commentary to 6:10—and either embrace her or him, or fall back to more comfortable arrangements.

In view of the promises of God, there is no reason to decline the venture. We have nothing finally to lose; if the self-giving that is love leads even to death, that too is overcome in advance, for we have died with Christ and may be certain of rising with him. The world will regularly recoil from love, but those who live amid the words and enacted signs of divine love, whether in synagogue or church, know supreme love, and therein know that also human love can serenely be accepted, indeed desired above all other created things. Readers should turn here to the commentary on 6:6–7.

Second, when love is accepted, the beloved brings peace. Love makes a new whole, within which satisfaction and animation are one. Does it always work that way? Apparently not. Need it ever not work that way? No.

8:11–12
His Own Vineyard

I

These verses make a complete poem, though they do seem to belong to a tradition or group of poems not otherwise represented in the Song. At least in the poem's present location, the speaker is the lover of the other poems. He is not, as otherwise in the Song, himself an honorific "Solomon"; rather in imagination he muses on and then addresses the Solomon of Israelite legend, concerning their respective vineyards. Also in this poem vineyards retain the potential for sexual metaphor that they carry elsewhere in the Song; here it is *possession* of vineyards that makes the metaphor. Solomon's vineyard, so large it has to be tended by servants—and apparently on shares!—must certainly be his famous harem. The lover brags to his imagined Solomon, "Keep your harem, for what it is worth! I have a vineyard that is my very own, and just for me." Solomon can have his many women; the lover has what Solomon will never have, unique union with his "vineyard."

There seems to have been no town named "Baal-hamon." The rabbis identified Baal-hamon as Jerusalem; if Solomon's "vineyard" is his harem, this must be right, whatever the basis of the identification (*Targum*).

99

II

We may begin by remembering that the historical Solomon's promiscuous sexual politics was the occasion of his promiscuity in the matter of gods, of his position as the first of the kings who "led Israel into idolatry." In the old stories about Solomon, the impossible size of his reputed harem is a sort of joke, but a joke of a very peculiar and dark kind: it is code for the limitlessness of idolatry once ventured. If two political wives with each their native god, why not four wives and four gods? Why not . . . ?

If we read the poem theologically, then it is the Lord who scorns Solomon as the lover does in the overt poem, and then Solomon is demoted from glory. Solomon becomes in the allegory a mere harem-keeping lord of this world, fit to be rebuked by the one faithful Lord—perhaps indeed Solomon is allegorically *the* "lord of this world." And two Israels appear: Israel as harem for the powers and principalities of this world, and Israel indissolubly and uniquely united to the one Lord.

It has always been so: old Israel and the synagogue and the church have always been both unfaithful and faithful; a collection of concubines for whoever is in power around them, and the bride uniquely taken by the Lord as his own. The contradiction will be resolved only eschatologically, when there are no more powers and principalities.

It may be appropriate to make a distinction suggested by the contrast of singular and plural in the above paragraph. It is as a group of individuals that the Lord's people go—in the prophets' image—whoring after other gods; it is the people as a singular entity, "the bride" in the Fathers' language or "the Assembly" in that of the rabbis, that is inalienably united with the Lord. There has been a long debate among Christians: Is it right to say that the church sins? The answer may borrow a famous distinction of social theory: as a *community* the church cannot sin, for as a community she is one person with the Lord, but as an *association*, as a collective of individuals each seeking his or her own in cooperation, the church can indeed be "a great sinner," as Martin Luther liked to chide her.

III

Some years ago a great basketball star told in print of his thousands of one-night women. One might have replied, with a tagline from a few decades ago: "Are you bragging or complaining?" For in truth, this "role model" thereby confessed to an awesome deprivation.

8:13
The Voice of Whom?

I

As in but one other case, 6:11–12, we can wrest from this verse no
overt sense, either because we lack a key or because it is a fragment
wholly dependent for its sense on the rest of a lost poem. The addressee
is a woman, which is as far as we get. Whether the speaker is the lover
or some other woman or someone else altogether, we cannot tell. Who
the "companions" are we cannot tell; the grammatical gender is masculine, which helps little. Several gardens have appeared in the Song;
we cannot tell whether this garden is one or none of them. And so on
through every bit of information we might need to unlock the text.

II

Since we can make out no overt sense, we can only repeat what we
said and did about the earlier passage. Theological exegesis can hardly
say a passage of canonical Scripture makes no sense at all, only that it
makes no sense to *us*. Moderns and late moderns occupy our own place
in hermeneutical history: we are required to begin from an overt sense.
If a text has none, we are stymied. This, however, does not mean that
the Spirit has not used passages closed to us, to enlighten believers of
other times, in their different place in hermeneutical history, or that he
will not do so again. Here as in the earlier case we will, instead of our
own commentary, simply offer a sample of what the Fathers, in their
very different hermeneutical situation, made of the verse.

The *glossa ordinaria*, the standard medieval exegetical compen-
dium, provided this allegory: "The church—or a faithful soul—dwells
in the gardens; she is already filled with the greenness of hope and good
works. The hope that this world breeds is dry and parched, for all the
things that people love here wither away swiftly. Hence she who dwells
in the gardens must make the Bridegroom hear her voice; that is, the
more her preaching speaks the good the more delighted is the One she
desires, because friends are listening, which is to say: all the elect desire
to hear the words of life" (Norris).

III

Under this rubric there is, as in the earlier case, nothing to be said.

8:14

Endings

I

Amid the general disorder of chapter 8, this verse may be just another swept-up fragment, and so ends the Song by happenstance and incoherently. Perhaps a commentator who has come to love the Song may be forgiven for hoping this is not the case, and so for seeking an alternative.

The verb in the first clause, *barah*, is translated by NRSV "make haste," so that the direction of the lover's running can, as suggested by the rest of the poem, be toward the woman. But it is translated by the *Targum* and all the ancient versions, "flee," so that his haste must be away from the woman. If with many commentators we follow this older and lexicographically perhaps easier translation, we will indeed have to regard this verse as a fragment, and one whose sense is lost with the rest of the poem. For from what is the lover to flee? To what? Why? We are told nothing.

Our verb might, however, be most strictly translated "be fleet"; and this is suggestive. It is indeed to flee that one more often needs to be *fleet*; notoriously, we are hardwired to "fight or flee," and to fight is to "stand and fight." It is this circumstance that tips the usage of such predicates as "be fleet"—and perhaps *barah*—toward "flee." But just so we may note that it is not always the case that it is flight which calls for being fleet—Greek legend's ideal warrior was called "Achilles-fleet-of-foot" for his *pursuit* of the enemy. The lover's haste need not be away from the woman, and the rest of the poem suggests the contrary. We will therefore stay with NRSV—and AV—and translate in neutral fashion. Then the unanswerable questions generated by "flee" vanish; and the verse can be read as a clear little poem—and as a perfect ending for the Song.

The woman speaks, and her speech carries the import of all her speeches in the Song: "Make haste [to me], my beloved." In that haste the beloved is as always to be like those sexually charged yet beautiful and innocent fauna of Eden whom we have met throughout the Song. And he is to make haste upon those mountains that sometimes represent the distance between them and sometimes are her most intimate sexual zone (4:1–7). Thus the Song ends with the same *eros* with which it began, but now filled with all the entreaty and promise and story sung on the way—and if this ending was not intended by author, editor, or canonizer, it can nevertheless be intended by Providence.

II

The Bible ends as the Song does. The most ancient recorded item of eucharistic liturgy is the church's entreaty for her risen Lord to *come*—and that quickly—to his bride gathered round the loaf and cup. So laden with power was the very sound of this cry that, even when the liturgy was otherwise in Greek, it in some places continued for a time to be uttered in the Aramaic of Jesus' first disciples: *maranatha*, "Come, Lord!" It is with this same eucharistic cry that the Christian Bible concludes: "Come, Lord Jesus!" (Rev. 22:20). John the Seer indeed knows the Lover's proper name, which the Song does not bring itself to speak; he appends a verse (22:21) assuring readers of the Lord's haste to answer the cry; and gives the "Amen." But with these glosses the Bible's ending only further displays its identity with that of the Song.

III

Let every lover say often to the beloved, "Make haste to me!" Let them even append some approximation of the Amen, "His advent is sure." Thus ends the song of the lovers, the song of the Lord and his bride, and the song of all human love, embedded as it is in the Song of God.

BIBLIOGRAPHY

For Further Study

Any who may want to dip further into the Song's exegesis will find the waters charted, to whatever depths they may wish to probe, by the Rev. Dr. John David Larsen's astonishing bibliographic labor of love, which covers both all surviving commentary on the Song, from the beginning to the present, *and* the scholarly work done on the most important ancient and medieval expositions. His work is—and may remain—unpublished, since he is constantly digging out additional obscure mentions of the Song, but the current version is obtainable from Dr. Larsen at Lutheran Campus Ministry, Rutgers University, New Brunswick, New Jersey.

Bernard of Clairvaux. *On the Song of Songs*. Trans. Kilian Walsh and Irene M. Edmunds. *The Works of Bernard of Clairvaux*, vols. 1–4. Kalamazoo, MI: Cistercian Publications, 1971–1980.

Davis, Ellen F. "Song of Songs." In *Proverbs, Ecclesiastes, and the Song of Songs*. Westminster Bible Companion. Louisville, KY: Westminster John Knox, 2000.

John of Ford. *Sermons on the Final Verses of the Song of Songs*. Trans. Wendy Mary Bekcett. Kalamazoo, MI: Cistercian Publications, 1977–1984.

Murphy, Roland E. *The Song of Songs: A Commentary on the Book of Canticles*. Hermeneia. Minneapolis: Fortress, 1990.

Nicholas of Lyra. *The Postilla of Nicholas of Lyra on the Song of Songs*. Ed. and trans. James George Kiecker. Milwaukee: Marquette University Press, 1998.

Norris, Richard A., ed. *The Song of Songs: Interpreted by Early Christian and Medieval Commentators*. The Church's Bible. Grand Rapids: Eerdmans, 2003.

Teresa of Avila. *Meditations on the Song of Songs. The Collected Works of St. Teresa of Avila*, vol. 2. Trans. Kieran Kavanaugh and Otilio Rodriguez. Washington, DC: Institute of Carmelite Studies, 1989.

Literature Cited

Bergant, Dianne, C.S.A. *The Song of Songs*. Berit Olam. Collegeville, MN: Liturgical Press, 2001.

Bernard of Clairvaux. *Sermones super Cantica canticorum*. Ed. Jean Leclerca, Charles H. Talbot, and Henri M. Rochais. Sancti Bernardi Opera. Rome: Editiones Cistercienses, 1957–1958.

———. *On the Song of Songs*. Trans. Kilian Walsh and Irene M. Edmunds. *The Works of Bernard of Clairvaux*, vols. 1–4. Kalamazoo, MI: Cistercian Publications, 1971–1980.

Davis, Ellen F. "Song of Songs." In *Proverbs, Ecclesiastes, and the Song of Songs*. Westminster Bible Companion. Louisville, KY: Westminster John Knox, 2000.

Gerlemann, Gillis. *Ruth, Das Hohelied*. Biblischer Kommentar Altes Testament, vol. 18. Neukirchen-Vluyn: Neukirchener, 1965.

Gregory of Nyssa. *Gregorii Nysseni in Canticum Canticorum*. Ed. Hermann Langerbeck. Gregorii Nysseni Opera, vol. 6. Leiden: Brill, 1960.

———. *Commentary on the Song of Songs*. Trans. Casimir McCambley. Brookline, MA: Hellenic College Press, 1987.

LaCocque, André. *Romance, She Wrote: A Hermeneutical Essay on Song of Songs*. Harrisburg, PA: Trinity Press International, 1998.

Longman, Tremper, III. *Song of Songs*. New International Commentary on the Old Testament. Grand Rapids: Eerdmans, 2001.

Murphy, Roland E. *The Song of Songs: A Commentary on the Book of Canticles*. Hermeneia. Minneapolis: Fortress, 1990.

Norris, Richard A., ed. *The Song of Songs: Interpreted by Early Christian and Medieval Commentators*. The Church's Bible. Grand Rapids: Eerdmans, 2003.

Origen. *Homiliae in Canticum canticorum* and *Commentarium in Canticum canticorum*. Ed. W. A. Baehrens. Die griechischen christlichen Schriftsteller der ersten drei Jahrhunderte, vol. 33. Leipzig, 1923.

———. *The Song of Songs Commentary and Homilies*. Trans. R. P. Lawson. Ancient Christian Writers, vol. 26. Westminster, MD: Newman, 1947.

Pope, Marvin H. *The Song of Songs: A New Translation with Introduction and Commentary*. Anchor Bible, vol. 7C. New York: Doubleday, 1977.

Song of Songs Rabbah. Trans. [Maurice] Simon. Midrash Rabbah. London: Soncino, 1930.

The Targum of Canticles. Trans. Philip S. Alexander. The Aramaic Bible. Collegeville, MN: Liturgical Press, 2003.